SLIMMIN
VEGETARI

By following the exciting
vegetarian menus in this boo
confidence in the knowledge that your body will be
getting all the nourishment it needs.

By the same author
VEGAN COOKING
VEGETARIAN PITTA BREAD RECIPES
THE SINGLE VEGAN

SLIMMING THE VEGETARIAN WAY

by

LEAH LENEMAN

THORSONS PUBLISHING GROUP

First published 1980

This revised and reset edition
published in 1989

© LEAH LENEMAN 1980

British Library Cataloguing in Publication Data

Leneman, Leah
Slimming the vegetarian way. – Rev. and
reset ed.
1. Slimmers: Vegetarians. Food – Recipes
I. Title
641.5'636

ISBN 0-7225-1587-1

*Published by Thorsons Publishers Limited,
Wellingborough, Northamptonshire, NN8 2RQ, England.*

Typeset by Harper Phototypesetters Limited, Northampton
Printed in Great Britain by Cox & Wyman Ltd, Reading, Berkshire

3   5   7   9   10   8   6   4   2

CONTENTS

The menus in this book are designed to cater for one person, and the daily calorie intake has been kept as near as possible to 1000 calories.

INTRODUCTION

The only sure way of losing weight is to cut down on calories. This immediately conjures up visions of deprivation, of having to forego all of the nicest things and eat only boring foods. It is this sense of deprivation and boredom which is the would-be slimmer's greatest enemy, and it is this which a vegetarian slimming diet can overcome.

Instead of the negative approach of lists of 'forbidden' foods, there is a positive attitude of new and adventurous eating. So, forget the old patterns and embark on something new — international menus offering novel tastes and textures. Not only will you lose weight while becoming fitter than ever, you will not feel bored, for one of the most important aspects of this vegetarian slimming diet is the enormous variety it offers.

Nutrition

Slimmers accustomed to eating meat may wonder if their bodies will be getting all the nutrients they are accustomed to. The answer is most emphatically yes. In fact, on a vegetarian slimming diet they should be getting more of these than ever before. In place of white bread and white rice, wholemeal bread and brown rice add extra nutrition and also the roughage so necessary for the slimmer.

Fresh fruit and vegetables and interesting salads are also included much more frequently than in many ordinary slimming diets, boosting vitamin and mineral intake in the nicest way possible. Nor is there any lack of protein. Cereals such as wheat and oats are combined with nuts and pulses in each day's menus to provide the amino acids which the body requires for protein building.

'Fattening' foods

Slimmers are accustomed to regarding certain foods as 'fattening'. In actual fact, no food is intrinsically fattening; some foods simply have a higher calorie count than others. This does not mean that all foods with a high calorie count should be avoided, for some of these are highly nutritious and play an important part in a vegetarian slimming diet. Nuts are the supreme example. Eaten as a between-meals snack they will undoubtedly help to put on weight, but incorporated as a protein source within a meal, they are not 'fattening' at all. This, of course, is the advantage of calorie counting; it allows items like nuts which are beneficial nutritionally, as well as delicious and filling, to be balanced with low calorie items for satisfying meals.

Pulses (beans and lentils) are also thought to be 'fattening' by some people, but considering their very high nutritional content and their satiety value, they are nothing of the kind. Baked beans on wholemeal toast, for example, provides a perfect combination of amino acids without undue calories.

'Starch' is something else which is labelled 'fattening'. If what is meant by 'starch' is white bread and rolls, crisps, sausage rolls and biscuits, then there is a strong element of truth in the claim, since most of these are so-called empty calories, i.e. they provide only the minimal amount of nutrients and because they contain so little substance they do not properly satisfy the body and consequently lead to overeating. But 'starch' in the form of unrefined cereals is another matter entirely.

Whole wheat really is the 'staff of life' — the 'germ' is high in protein while the bran provides the essential roughage. There is no need to take bran separately, the menus which follow contain all the roughage needed in a much more palatable form. Oats have an even higher protein content than wheat, and rye is also valuable.

('Brown' rye crispbread is specified in the menus because the lighter variety provides less bulk with no fewer calories.)

Another slimming bête-noire is pasta. In fact, wholemeal spaghetti and macaroni are nourishing and satisfying and not at all high in calories. Ordinary pasta is less substantial, but being made from durum wheat it does contain a significant amount of protein. The main problem with eating pasta dishes in restaurants (and this goes for curries and some Chinese meals as well) is the large amount of oil used in their preparation.

Fats are far and away the highest calorie item in any diet, and a careful watch must be kept on these. (There are, of course, low-fat spreads which contain approximately half the calories of butter or margarine, but these cannot be used for cooking.) On the other hand, it is a mistake to attempt to exclude all fats from the diet since pure vegetable oils and most vegetable margarines are poly-unsaturates which the body needs, and these are therefore included — in small amounts of course — in a vegetarian slimming diet.

For both health and ethical reasons, more and more people are turning to low-dairy or non-dairy vegetarian diets. Skimmed milk is free of saturated fat, but so is soya milk, which is not very much higher in calories and has considerably more body.

Meals

A reasonably substantial breakfast is a must for anyone who wants to avoid mid-morning snacks. Eggs are for this reason a popular choice, but as with all animal products, it is best to eat these only occasionally. Vegan alternatives are provided for all egg-based breakfasts.

Cereals of various kinds are the most convenient breakfast, particularly when there is not much time for preparation. Certain brand names are specifically mentioned (Shredded Wheat, Weetabix and Grape Nuts) because they are made from whole wheat. Muesli-type cereals are now available in supermarkets, but for the most part these contain excessive amounts of sugar; the health store varieties are therefore to be preferred. Granola is a kind of toasted muesli, delicious and substantial. Also, fresh seasonal fruit, or fruit juice, should form part of every breakfast.

Soup is a useful lunch in cold weather because it can be really filling without being high in calories. The ideal lunch is a salad, but as the aim of the menus is to provide as much variety as possible, salads are not included on a daily basis. On days when salad is not on the menu it is a good idea to sprinkle cress or chopped parsley over the soup or evening savoury. Sprouted beans and alfalfa are wonderful raw foods; they are rich in vitamins and minerals as well as protein and can be sprinkled over savouries or incorporated into salads. The beans or alfalfa seeds should be placed in a glass jar (only a small quantity as the size multiplies many times over). A strip of gauze, obtainable from any chemist, is cut to size and attached by rubber band to the top of the jar. The beans are covered with lukewarm water and left to soak overnight (alfalfa only needs a couple of hours). They should then be drained thoroughly and the jar placed on its side in a warm spot. Every morning and evening rinse the sprouts and leave them to drain until they have sprouted and are ready for eating (the bean is eaten as well as the sprout).

Most of the evening meals are self-contained — in other words they do not require a separate vegetable accompaniment (those recipes which do require one specifically mention this and include the calorie content of the vegetable). This makes for maximum convenience, particularly if only one member of a family is following the menus. But although recipes are for one portion they can easily be doubled or quadrupled, and they are piquant and sustaining enough to serve even the most discriminating of guests (though for non-slimmers with big appetites do prepare larger portions).

Lunches and dinners may be reversed, and this is actually quite a good idea since the body will then have more time to burn off the larger amount of calories. The meals have been given in the conventional form of the larger evening meal simply because this is what suits most people. Although meals in any one day may be reversed, individual meals should not be transposed from one day's menu to another even if the calorie count is similar, because the meals on any one day have been planned to balance each other (for example, a low-protein evening meal would be complemented by a high protein breakfast and lunch).

Beverages are not specifically mentioned in the menus. Tea and coffee have no nutritional value, and milk and sugar add extra calories which cannot be afforded. Pure spring water (available from health food stores) is the most refreshing drink there is, and for a hot drink herb teas are highly recommended. They are soothing and comforting, and as they do not require milk and sugar they are virtually calorie free. If the bitter taste of coffee is missed, then one of the coffee substitutes available at health food stores can be taken black and unsweetened. If the tea habit is too hard to break, then weak China tea without milk or sugar is the least harmful. Alcoholic drinks, like sugar, contain empty calories and, furthermore, they stimulate the appetite; alcohol therefore does not belong in a slimming diet.

The sweet tooth

Saccharin and chemical sweeteners are not recommended because the long-term effects are still not known and because this diet is based on natural foods rather than synthetics. A short section of low-calorie puddings without artificial sweeteners will be found after the menus; they are really for special occasions when you wish to serve a sweet but do not want to completely wreck your diet. No sweets are included in the actual menus since on a 1000 calorie diet it is important that only the most nutritious foods be taken, and there is no real place for sweets.

The one meal where a small quantity of sugar or honey appears fairly regularly is breakfast since the body is able to burn this off during the day. The sweet tooth is also catered for in the section on 'crash' diets.

PREFACE
TO THE NEW EDITION

The first thing that anyone in possession of the previous edition will doubtless notice is that the calorie totals of many of the existing meals have changed. There are three main reasons for this. The first is that teaspoons and tablespoons are now in accord with international measures of 5mls and 15mls. The second is my discovery that two teaspoons of vegetable oil is quite sufficient for sautéeing vegetables, which has enabled me to shave calories off most menus. And the third is that I used a different set of calorie books this time, which provided different figures for certain foods (the calorie chart at the end of the book has been updated accordingly). I can promise, however, that the changes are not significant enough to have adversely affected anyone who followed the previous edition.

Indeed, it seems worth emphasizing that to be 100 per cent accurate in counting calories is a virtual impossibility. I based most calorie amounts on an ounce measure; this is given as 25 grams for simplicity, but in reality an ounce is 28 grams, so by the time you get to 4 ounces there is already a disparity. Similarly, conversions to American cups cannot possibly be perfectly precise. At this level, though, it quite simply does not matter.

For those who like to know such things, but do not want to have to work them out from the calorie chart, I considered a small onion to be 2 ounces (one could always buy a large one and chop off 2 oz chunks as needed), and a small carrot to be the same, while a small green pepper was 6 ounces.

While on the subject of weighing, I would highly recommend a particular set of kitchen scales currently on the British market,

Salter's Diet 32. It is the only set I know of on which one can easily weigh ¼ oz.

Not that there is any point in being fanatical. If an onion is 3 ounces or a green pepper 8 ounces, it is not going to make the slightest difference. It is only in the area of fats that the slimmer has to be really careful, since a single teaspoon adds 40 calories to the meal.

One ingredient which did not appear in the previous edition but features in a number of new recipes — as an alternative to Parmesan cheese — is nutritional yeast. Brewer's yeast has never appealed, but since discovering Good Tasting Yeast (which can be ordered direct from The Good Tasting Food Co., P.O. Box 188, Summertown, TN 38483, USA) I am a great convert to this highly nutritious food. I understand there are now autolized yeast flakes available in Britain which are also very palatable.

The greatest change which has occurred since the first edition of this book appeared has been the phenomenal proliferation of soya foods (soyfoods in American parlance). Tofu is arguably the best friend a slimmer ever had, for no other food so low in calories and high in protein is as versatile as tofu. Tempeh is another fine soya food for slimmers, though as it is not as readily available as tofu, I have confined its use to only one recipe. Since soya milk and yogurt are now so easy to obtain, I have given them as alternatives to the dairy versions, so that vegans, and others trying to cut down on dairy produce, will be able to use the book in the same way as lacto-vegetarians.

The new menus aim to provide even greater variety for slimmers who decide to try the vegetarian way.

SPRING MENUS

MENU 1

Breakfast

Imperial (Metric)	American	Calories
2 oz (50g) muesli	½ cup muesli	220
¼ pint (150ml) skimmed milk or 4 fl oz (100ml) soya milk	⅔ cup skim milk or ½ cup soymilk	50
1 medium-sized apple, chopped or grated	1 small apple, chopped or grated	50
		320

Lunch

PULSE AND CABBAGE SOUP

Imperial (Metric)	American	Calories
1 oz (25g) black-eyed beans	1 ounce black-eyed peas	85
1 oz (25g) green or brown lentils	1 ounce green or brown lentils	75
8 fl oz (225ml) water	1 cup water	
4 oz (100g) cabbage	¼ pound cabbage	30
garlic salt and chopped fresh or dried mint to taste	garlic salt and chopped fresh or dried mint to taste	
		190

Cover beans and lentils with boiling water and soak overnight. Drain, add fresh water and bring to the boil. Finely chop the cabbage and add to the pot. Cook gently for 30 minutes. Add seasoning to taste and serve.

Dinner

CASHEW RISOTTO

Imperial (Metric)	American	Calories
1½ oz (40g) long-grain brown rice	¼ cup long-grain brown rice	150
4 oz (100g) tinned tomatoes	4 ounces canned tomatoes	12
1 small onion	1 small onion	12
1 oz (25g) broken cashew nuts	¼ cup chopped cashews	175
2 teaspoons vegetable oil	2 teaspoons vegetable oil	80
½ green pepper	½ green pepper	16
4 oz (100g) mushrooms	2 cups mushrooms	10
½ teaspoon marjoram or basil	½ teaspoon marjoram or basil	
salt and pepper to taste	salt and pepper to taste	
		455
	Total	965

Cover rice with boiling water and soak overnight. Drain well. Chop onion, green pepper and mushrooms. Fry in oil for 5 minutes. Add rice and stir well. Add tomatoes and herbs (plus a little more liquid if necessary during cooking). Simmer over low heat until rice is tender and liquid is absorbed (about 25 minutes). Meanwhile, toast the cashew pieces and mix them in when the rice is ready to serve.

MENU 2

Breakfast

Imperial (Metric)	American	Calories
4 fl oz (100ml) unsweetened orange juice	½ cup orange juice	40
scrambled egg made with 1 large egg and a few drops skimmed milk; or scrambled tofu made by mashing 3 oz (75g) tofu with 1 teaspoon soya sauce and a pinch of turmeric	scrambled egg made with 1 large egg and a few drops skim milk; or scrambled tofu made by mashing 3 ounces tofu with 1 teaspoon soy sauce and a pinch of turmeric	95
cooked in 1½ teaspoons vegetable margarine	cooked in 1½ teaspoons vegetable margarine	60
and served on 1 small slice wholemeal toast	and served on 1 small slice wholewheat toast	65
		260

Lunch

MIXED SALAD

Imperial (Metric)	American	Calories
(lettuce	(lettuce	
tomatoes	tomatoes	
cucumber	cucumber	
grated carrot	grated carrot	
spring onion)	scallion)	20
topped with 1 oz (25g) hazelnuts, toasted and ground	topped with ¼ cup hazelnuts, toasted and ground	180
served with 1 slice brown rye crispbread, thinly spread with butter or vegetable margarine	served with 1 slice brown rye crispbread, thinly spread with butter or vegetable margarine	60
		260

Dinner

ORIENTAL SPAGHETTI

Imperial (Metric)	American	Calories
1 small carrot	1 small carrot	10
1 small green pepper	1 small green pepper	24
2 oz (50g) wholemeal spaghetti	2 ounces wholewheat spaghetti	200
1 oz (25g) almonds	¼ cup almonds	160
1 small onion	1 small onion	12
2 oz (50g) mushrooms	1 cup mushrooms	5
2 teaspoons vegetable oil	2 teaspoons vegetable oil	80
Tamari (soya sauce) to taste	Tamari (soy sauce) to taste	
		491
	Total	1011

Put spaghetti on to cook in boiling water. Slice the carrot lengthwise into thin sticks. Chop the onion, slice the green pepper and mushrooms. *Sauté* the vegetables and almonds in the oil in a large frying pan over moderate heat until just tender. When the spaghetti is cooked drain it and add it to the frying pan with the tamari. Stir the mixture together over moderate heat for approximately 3 minutes and serve.

MENU 3

Breakfast

SUNSHINE SPECIAL

Imperial (Metric)	American	Calories
1 oz (25g) rolled oats	¼ cup rolled oats	105
1 oz (25g) raisins	⅙ cup raisins	75
½ oz (15g) brown sugar	½ ounce brown sugar	50
1 oz (25g) wholewheat flakes	1 ounce wholewheat flakes	100
½ oz (15g) almonds, chopped	⅛ cup almonds, chopped	85
1 apple, chopped	1 small apple, chopped	50
½ oz (15g) desiccated coconut	⅙ cup grated coconut	90
¼ pint (150ml) skimmed milk or 4 fl oz (100ml) soya milk	⅔ cup skim milk or ½ cup soymilk	50
		605

Combine dry ingredients. Top with chopped apple and milk.

Lunch

BAKED BEANS ON TOAST

Imperial (Metric)	American	Calories
5 oz (150g) tinned baked beans	5 ounces canned vegetarian baked beans	130
2 small unbuttered slices wholemeal toast	2 small unbuttered slices wholewheat toast	130
		260

Heat baked beans and serve on toast.

Dinner

VEGETABLE RAGOUT

Imperial (Metric)	American	Calories
1 small green pepper	1 small green pepper	24
1 onion	1 onion	
1 small clove garlic }	1 small clove garlic }	24
2 carrots	2 carrots	
1 bay leaf	1 bay leaf	
½ teaspoon basil	½ teaspoon basil	
4 oz (100g) tomatoes	¼ pound tomatoes	15
½ pint (150ml) water	1⅓ cups water	
½ vegetable stock cube	½ vegetable stock cube	15
1 small turnip	1 small turnip	12
2 sticks celery	2 stalks celery	5
2 teaspoons vegetable oil	2 teaspoons vegetable oil	80
salt and pepper to taste	salt and pepper to taste	
		175
	Total	1040

Chop onion, pepper and garlic finely and fry for five minutes in the oil with the bay leaf and basil. Slice carrots, turnips and celery into small pieces, add to onion mixture, pour in water and add half a stock cube. Bring to boiling point and simmer for 20-30 minutes until vegetables are just tender. Add salt to taste. Top with tomatoes which have been quartered.

MENU 4

Breakfast

Imperial (Metric)	American	Calories
4 fl oz (100ml) unsweetened orange juice	½ cup orange juice	40
2 oz (50g) Grapenuts served with:	½ cup Grapenuts served with:	200
¼ pint (150ml) skimmed milk or 4 fl oz (100ml) soya milk	⅔ cup skim milk or ½ cup soymilk	50
½ oz (15g) brown sugar or ¾ oz (20g) honey	½ ounce brown sugar or ¾ ounce honey	60
		350

Lunch

SPROUTED CHICK PEA (GARBANZO BEAN) SALAD

Imperial (Metric)	American	Calories
1 oz (25g) chick peas (sprouted according to instructions in introduction)	⅛ cup garbanzo beans (sprouted according to instructions in introduction)	90
1 tablespoon chopped parsley	1 tablespoon chopped parsley	
2 teaspoons cider vinegar	2 teaspoons cider vinegar	
1 spring onion } 1 tomato	1 scallion } 1 small tomato	10
1 tablespoon vegetable oil	1 tablespoon vegetable oil	110
garlic salt and pepper to taste	garlic salt and pepper to taste	
2 thin slices wholemeal bread with a thin scraping of butter or vegetable margarine	2 thin slices wholewheat bread with a thin scraping of butter or vegetable margarine	200
		410

Chop spring onion (scallion) and tomato. Combine with chick peas (garbanzo beans) and parsley. Mix together oil and vinegar with seasoning to taste and toss dressing with salad. Serve with the slices of wholemeal bread.

Dinner

VEGETABLE STUFFED AUBERGINE (EGGPLANT)

Imperial (Metric)	American	Calories
8 oz (225g) aubergine	½ pound eggplant	32
1 onion	1 small onion	12
2 teaspoons vegetable oil	2 teaspoons vegetable oil	80
1 small green pepper	1 small green pepper	24
1 stick celery	1 stalk celery	5
2 tomatoes	2 small tomatoes	20
2 oz (50g) mushrooms	1 cup mushrooms	5
salt and pepper	salt and pepper	
1 teaspoon brown sugar	1 teaspoon raw sugar	17
1 teaspoon marjoram	1 teaspoon marjoram	
4 fl oz (100ml) tomato juice	½ cup tomato juice	25
		220
	Total	980

Cook the aubergine (eggplant) whole in boiling water for 10 minutes. Drain. Skin the tomatoes and chop all the vegetables. *Sauté* the onion in the oil until becoming tender, then add the rest of the vegetables and seasonings and cook for 10 minutes. Cut the aubergine (eggplant) in half, scoop out the centre and chop. Mix it into the onion mixture and stuff the shell. Arrange in a baking dish, top with tomato juice, and pour in a little water in the bottom of the dish to prevent the aubergine (eggplant) burning. Cover and bake at 350°F (180°C/Gas Mark 4) for 30 minutes.

MENU 5

Breakfast

Imperial (Metric)	American	Calories
1½ oz (40g) Granola type cereal	⅓ cup Granola	200
served with:	served with:	
¼ pint (150ml) skimmed milk or 4 fl oz (100ml) soya milk	⅔ cup skim milk or ½ cup soymilk	50
1 sliced banana	1 sliced banana	60
		310

Lunch

SWEET AND SOUR CABBAGE SOUP

Imperial (Metric)	American	Calories
4 oz (100g) cabbage	¼ pound cabbage	24
1 small onion	1 small onion	12
4 oz (100g) tinned tomatoes	4 ounces canned tomatoes	12
2 oz (50g) dairy or soya yogurt	¼ cup dairy or soy yogurt	30
1 teaspoon lemon juice (or more to taste)	1 teaspoon lemon juice (or more to taste)	
1 heaped teaspoon brown sugar	1 heaped teaspoon brown sugar	30
½ pint (225ml) water	1⅓ cups water	
salt and pepper to taste	salt and pepper to taste	
2 slices brown rye crispbread (unbuttered)	2 slices brown rye crispbread (unbuttered)	50
		158

Shred the cabbage finely, dice the onion and add both to boiling water. Simmer for 20 minutes. Add the rest of the ingredients (except the yogurt). Simmer for 45 minutes to an hour. Taste from time to time and correct seasonings to taste. Serve topped with yogurt and accompanied by the crispbread.

Dinner

MACARONI AND CASHEW SAVOURY

Imperial (Metric)	American	Calories
2 oz (50g) wholemeal macaroni	½ cup wholewheat macaroni	200
1 oz (25g) ground cashews	¼ cup ground cashews	180
1 small onion	1 small onion	12
2 tomatoes	2 small tomatoes	20
1 Shredded Wheat biscuit	1 Shredded Wheat biscuit	85
1 teaspoon celery salt	1 teaspoon celery salt	
		497
	Total	965

Chop the onion finely and cook with the macaroni in enough water to cover. When the macaroni is done, drain and crumble the shredded wheat into this. Skin and chop the tomatoes and add them with the nuts and seasoning to the macaroni mixture. Bake for half an hour in a moderate oven; 350°F (180°C/Gas Mark 4).

MENU 6

Breakfast

Imperial (Metric)	American	Calories
4 fl oz (100ml) unsweetened grapefruit juice	½ cup grapefruit juice	35
1 poached egg or 3 oz (75g) firm tofu, thinly sliced and grilled on each side	1 poached egg or 3 ounces firm tofu, thinly sliced and broiled on each side	90
1 small tomato, sliced	2½ ounces tomato slices	10
2 oz (50g) grilled mushrooms	1 cup broiled mushrooms	5
1 slice lightly buttered wholemeal toast	1 slice lightly buttered wholewheat toast	90
		230

Lunch

ARTICHOKE SALAD

Imperial (Metric)	American	Calories
¼ cucumber	¼ cucumber	5
lettuce leaves	lettuce leaves	
½ small green pepper	½ small green pepper	12
4 oz (100g) tinned artichoke hearts	4 ounces canned artichoke hearts	30
1 oz (25g) walnut pieces	¼ cup walnut pieces	150
2 oz (50g) button mushrooms	1 cup button mushrooms	5
1 tablespoon vegetable oil	1 tablespoon vegetable oil	120
1 teaspoon lemon juice	1 teaspoon lemon juice	
		322

Wash and thinly slice cucumber, green pepper and raw mushrooms. Arrange on lettuce leaves with halved artichoke hearts. Combine oil and lemon juice and sprinkle over the salad. Top with walnuts.

Dinner

CREOLE SUPPER

Imperial (Metric)	American	Calories
1 oz (25g) unflavoured mince style TVP	1 ounce unflavoured mince style TVP	95
1 teaspoon yeast extract	1 teaspoon yeast extract	5
1 small onion	1 small onion	12
½ teaspoon cayenne pepper	½ teaspoon cayenne pepper	
2 teaspoons vegetable oil	2 teaspoons vegetable oil	80
1 teaspoon salt	1 teaspoon salt	
1 teaspoon brown sugar	1 teaspoon brown sugar	17
½ small green pepper	½ small green pepper	12
2 oz (50g) long-grain brown rice	⅓ cup brown rice	200
4 oz (100g) tinned tomatoes	4 ounces canned tomatoes	12
		433
	Total	985

In the morning, cover the rice with boiling water and leave to soak. Drain and cook in lightly salted water. Chop onion and green pepper, fry until tender then add tomatoes and seasonings. Cover TVP with enough hot water to moisten thoroughly, mixing in yeast extract at the same time. When rice is nearly done, mix TVP in with the tomato mixture, adding more water if it is too dry. Pile rice on plate and TVP mixture on top.

MENU 7

Breakfast

Imperial (Metric)	American	Calories
¼ cup (150ml) orange juice	⅔ cup orange juice	50
scrambled egg made with 1 large egg and a few drops skimmed milk; or scrambled tofu made by mashing 3 oz (75g) tofu with 1 teaspoon soya sauce and pinch turmeric	scrambled egg made with 1 large egg and a few drops skim milk; or scrambled tofu made by mashing 3 ounces tofu with 1 teaspoon soy sauce and pinch turmeric	95
1½ teaspoons vegetable margarine	1½ teaspoons vegetable margarine	60
1 large slice wholemeal bread	1 large slice wholewheat bread	75
		280

Lunch

LEEK AND LEMON SOUP

Imperial (Metric)	American	Calories
1 small leek	1 small leek	25
2 teaspoons vegetable oil	2 teaspoons vegetable oil	80
1 heaped teaspoon wholemeal flour	1 heaped teaspoon wholewheat flour	30
½ pint (225ml) water	1⅓ cups water	
½ vegetable stock cube	½ vegetable stock cube	15
rind and juice of ½ small lemon	rind and juice of ½ small lemon	
1 small onion } ½ clove garlic }	1 small onion } ½ clove garlic }	15
½ teaspoon grated nutmeg	½ teaspoon grated nutmeg	
salt and pepper to taste	salt and pepper to taste	
2 brown rye crispbreads (unbuttered)	2 brown rye crispbreads (unbuttered)	50
		215

Wash and slice leek. Heat oil and fry leek for 2-3 minutes. Stir in flour and cook for 2 minutes. Blend in water, add stock cube and bring to the boil. Grate onion, crush garlic, add both to soup, as well as rind and juice of lemon, nutmeg and seasoning. Stir thoroughly. Simmer for 45 minutes. Serve with crispbread.

Dinner

CARROT AND HAZELNUT RISOTTO

Imperial (Metric)	American	Calories
1 oz (25g) hazelnuts	¼ cup hazelnuts	180
1 small onion	1 small onion	12
2 teaspoons vegetable oil	2 teaspoons vegetable oil	80
1 small carrot	1 small carrot	12
2 oz (50g) mushrooms	1 cup mushrooms	5
2 oz (50g) long-grain brown rice	⅓ cup brown rice	200
salt, pepper and paprika	salt, pepper and paprika	
		489
	Total	984

Cover the rice with boiling water in the morning and leave to soak. Drain and cook in boiling salted water to cover. Place the hazelnuts under a grill (broiler), turning frequently. When they are nicely roasted cool them then rub the outer skins off and discard. Coarsely grind the nuts and set aside. Chop the onion and *sauté* in the oil until tender, grate the carrot, slice the mushrooms and add both to the onion. Cook together for a few minutes then add it to the rice with the seasonings, simmer briefly and dish up. Top with the ground hazelnuts.

MENU 8

Breakfast

Imperial (Metric)	American	Calories
2 oz (50g) Muesli	½ cup Muesli	220
¼ pint (150ml) skimmed milk or 4 fl oz (100ml) soya milk	⅔ cup skim milk or ½ cup soymilk	50
1 medium-sized orange, segmented	1 medium-sized orange, segmented	50
		320

Lunch

BRUSSELS SPROUTS SALAD

Imperial (Metric)	American	Calories
4 oz (100g) Brussels sprouts	¼ pound Brussels sprouts	28
1 stick celery	1 stalk celery	5
1 small carrot	1 small carrot	12
1 apple	1 small apple	50
2 oz (50g) dairy or soya yogurt	¼ cup dairy or soy yogurt	30
½ punnet of mustard and cress	a little cress	3
1 oz (25g) walnuts	¼ cup walnuts	150
½ teaspoon lemon juice	½ teaspoon lemon juice	
		278

Grate the sprouts, carrot and apple. Chop the celery. Mix together with walnuts, yogurt and lemon juice and serve topped with cress.

Dinner

MUSHROOM AND CASHEW SAVOURY

Imperial (Metric)	American	Calories
1½ oz (40g) cashew nuts	⅓ cup cashews	270
2 oz (50g) mushrooms	1 cup mushrooms	5
2 teaspoons vegetable oil	2 teaspoons vegetable oil	80
½ teaspoon yeast extract	½ teaspoon yeast extract	5
1 small onion	1 small onion	12
1 small tomato	2½ ounce tomato	12
1 teaspoon wholemeal flour	1 teaspoon wholewheat flour	25
½ teaspoon thyme	½ teaspoon thyme	
		409
	Total	1007

Slice onion, mushrooms and tomato and *sauté* gently in oil.
Meanwhile, toast the cashews under the grill until lightly browned.
When the onions are tender, stir in flour and cook for 2-3 minutes.
Slowly add enough water to make a thick sauce, stirring constantly.
Add yeast extract, thyme and cashews and mix well.

MENU 9

Breakfast

OAT AND SEED CEREAL

Imperial (Metric)	American	Calories
1½ oz (40g) rolled oats	⅓ cup rolled oats	160
1 oz (25g) sunflower seeds	¼ cup sunflower seeds	170
1½ tablespoons clear honey	1½ tablespoons clear honey	60
¼ pint (150ml) skimmed milk or 4 fl oz (100ml) soya milk	⅔ cup skim milk or ½ cup soymilk	50
1 oz (25g) raisins	⅙ cup raisins	70
1 small pear	1 small pear	40
		550

Lunch

CURRIED CARROT SOUP

Imperial (Metric)	American	Calories
1 small onion	1 small onion	12
1½ teaspoons vegetable margarine	1½ teaspoons vegetable margarine	60
¼ pint vegetable stock	⅔ cup vegetable stock	
½ teaspoon curry powder (or more to taste)	½ teaspoon curry powder (or more to taste)	
4 oz (100g) carrots	¼ pound carrots	24
		96

Melt margarine and *sauté* chopped onions. Add curry powder and cook another minute. Slice the carrots and add them with the stock. Bring to the boil and cook until the carrots are tender. Put in liquidizer and blend thoroughly. Reheat briefly.

Dinner

BAKED NOODLES AND MUSHROOMS

Imperial (Metric)	American	Calories
2 oz (50g) wholemeal noodles	2 ounces wholewheat noodles	200
2 oz (50g) mushrooms	1 cup mushrooms	5
1 tablespoon Tamari (soya sauce)	1 tablespoon Tamari (soy sauce)	5
1 small onion	1 small onion	12
1 heaped teaspoon wholemeal flour	1 heaped teaspoon wholewheat flour	30
2 teaspoons vegetable oil	2 teaspoons vegetable oil	80
4 oz (100g) spring cabbage	¼ pound spring cabbage	24
		356
	Total	1002

Cook noodles in salted, boiling water until tender. Chop onion and mushrooms and *sauté* in oil until tender. Sprinkle with flour and cook together for 2 minutes. Slowly add tamari and just enough water to make a fairly thick sauce. Put noodles in casserole dish and pour mushroom sauce over the top. Bake for 20-30 minutes at 350°F (180°C/Gas Mark 4). Serve with the spring cabbage, chopped and lightly steamed.

MENU 10

Breakfast

Imperial (Metric)	American	Calories
2 oz (50g) grapes	2 ounces grapes	30

TOMATOES ON TOAST

Imperial (Metric)	American	Calories
6 oz (175g) tomatoes	6 ounces tomatoes	24
2 teaspoons vegetable margarine	2 teaspoons vegetable margarine	80
salt and pepper	salt and pepper	
2 small slices wholemeal toast	2 small slices wholewheat toast	130
		264

Chop the tomatoes coarsely. Heat the margarine in a frying pan and cook the tomatoes until they are nice and soft. Season well with lots of freshly ground black pepper. Serve piled onto the toast.

Lunch

PINEAPPLE TOFU SALAD

Imperial (Metric)	American	Calories
4 oz (100g) firm tofu	½ cup firm tofu	116
1 oz (25g) dairy or soya yogurt	⅛ cup dairy or soy yogurt	15
pinch sea salt	pinch sea salt	
1 oz (25g) dates	1 ounce dates	70
½ oz (15g) walnuts	⅛ cup walnuts	75
2 slices fresh pineapple	2 slices fresh pineapple	60
		336

Drain the tofu, place it in a bowl and mash it. Mix in the yogurt and salt. Chop the dates and walnuts coarsely. Mix in with the tofu. Core the pineapple slices. Pile the tofu mixture in the centres.

Dinner

CARROT AND OLIVE RICE SAVOURY

Imperial (Metric)	American	Calories
3 oz (75g) brown rice	½ cup brown rice	300
3 oz (75g) carrots	3 ounces carrots	18
3 tablespoons hot water	3 tablespoons hot water	
8 black olives	8 black olives	40
½ teaspoon onion salt	½ teaspoon onion salt	
2 teaspoons lemon juice	2 teaspoons lemon juice	
2 teaspoons Parmesan cheese or nutritional yeast	2 teaspoons Parmesan cheese or nutritional yeast	25
4 oz (100g) broccoli	¼ pound broccoli	24
		407
	Total	1007

Cook the rice until tender. Grate the carrots. Cover them with the water in a small saucepan and cook for 4-5 minutes. Chop the olives finely. Combine the carrots with their cooking water, rice, olives, onion salt, lemon juice, and the cheese or yeast. Bake the mixture at 325°F (170°C/Gas Mark 3) for about half an hour. Serve accompanied by lightly-steamed broccoli.

MENU 11

Breakfast

Imperial (Metric)	American	Calories
1 passion fruit	1 passion fruit	10

CRISPBREAD WITH GRILLED (BROILED) PEANUT BUTTER AND HONEY

Imperial (Metric)	American	Calories
2 brown rye crispbreads	2 brown rye crispbreads	50
1 tablespoon peanut butter	1 tablespoon peanut butter	90
2 tablespoons honey	2 tablespoons honey	80
		230

To eat the passion fruit, slice the top off and eat the inside with a teaspoon.

Mix the peanut butter and honey in a small bowl. Spread on the crispbread. Place the crispbreads with their topping under the grill (broiler) and cook until the topping is lightly browned and bubbling.

Lunch

MIDDLE-EASTERN BULGUR WHEAT SALAD

Imperial (Metric)	American	Calories
2 oz (50g) bulgur wheat	⅓ cup bulgur wheat	200
1 small onion	1 small onion	12
2 teaspoons vegetable oil	2 teaspoons vegetable oil	80
2 tablespoons tomato purée	2 tablespoons tomato paste	20
½ oz (15g) walnuts	⅛ cup walnuts	75
1 teaspoon minced parsley	1 teaspoon minced parsley	
½ teaspoon dried oregano	½ teaspoon dried oregano	
¼ teaspoon ground cumin	¼ teaspoon ground cumin	
¼ teaspoon ground coriander	¼ teaspoon ground coriander	

pinch cinnamon   pinch cinnamon
pinch cayenne pepper   pinch cayenne pepper
                                                    _____
                                                      387

Cover the wheat with cold water and leave for half an hour or
more. Drain well in a sieve, squeezing it down to get rid of excess
moisture. Chop the onion. *Sauté* in the oil until just beginning to
brown. Add the onion to the wheat, along with all the other
ingredients, and mix well. Chill for an hour or longer before
serving.

Dinner

TOFU CELERY LOAF

Imperial (Metric)	American	Calories
1 oz (25g) brown rice	¹⁄₆ cup brown rice	100
4 oz (100g) firm tofu	½ cup firm tofu	116
1 oz (25g) fresh wholemeal breadcrumbs	½ cup fresh wholewheat breadcrumbs	65
1 stick celery	1 stalk celery	5
1 tablespoon tahini	1 tablespoon tahini	90
juice of ½ small lemon	juice of ½ small lemon	
1 tablespoon Tamari (soya sauce)	1 tablespoon Tamari (soy sauce)	5
4 oz (100g) spring cabbage	¼ pound spring cabbage	12
		393
	Total	1010

Cook the rice until tender. Mash the tofu in a bowl. Chop the
celery finely. Add it to the tofu, along with the rice, breadcrumbs,
tahini, lemon juice, and Tamari. Mix well. Transfer to a small loaf
pan or baking dish, and bake at 375°F (190°C/Gas Mark 5) for
25-30 minutes. Serve accompanied by the spring cabbage, lightly
steamed.

MENU 12

Breakfast

Imperial (Metric)	American	Calories
4 fl oz (100ml) grapefruit juice	½ cup grapefruit juice	35
3 oatcakes	3 oatcakes	180
1 tablespoon peanut butter	1 tablespoon peanut butter	90
2 teaspoons raw sugar or sugar-free jam	2 teaspoons raw sugar or sugar-free jam	34
		339

Spread the peanut butter on the oatcakes, and the jam on top of the peanut butter.

Lunch

MIDDLE-EASTERN ROASTED GREEN PEPPER SALAD

Imperial (Metric)	American	Calories
1 medium green pepper	1 medium green pepper	24
2 teaspoons cider vinegar	2 teaspoons cider vinegar	
2 teaspoons olive oil	2 teaspoons olive oil	80
½ clove garlic	½ clove garlic	
salt and pepper	salt and pepper	
1 slice wholemeal bread, thinly spread with butter or vegetable margarine	1 slice wholewheat bread, thinly spread with butter or vegetable margarine	100
		204

Quarter the pepper. Place under a hot grill (broiler) with the shiny side (outside) of the pepper facing the heat. Grill (broil) until the pepper quarters are all thoroughly blackened on top. (It may be necessary to move them around under the heat in order to achieve this.) Cool, then peel off the skins and cut the peppers into strips. Crush the garlic. Combine the vinegar, oil, garlic and seasoning to taste, and sprinkle over the pepper strips. Serve chilled, accompanied by the bread.

Dinner

CHICK PEA (GARBANZO BEAN) AND NOODLE CASSEROLE

Imperial (Metric)	American	Calories
2 oz (50g) wholemeal noodles	2 ounces wholewheat noodles	200
1 small onion	1 small onion	12
1 stick celery	1 stalk celery	5
2 teaspoons vegetable oil	2 teaspoons vegetable oil	80
2 oz (50g) mushrooms	1 cup mushrooms	5
2 teaspoons wholemeal flour	2 teaspoons wholewheat flour	35
¼ pint (150ml) skimmed milk or 4 fl oz (100ml) soya milk	⅔ cup skim milk or ½ cup soymilk	50
4 oz (100g) cooked chick peas	4 ounces cooked garbanzo beans	104
½ teaspoon dried marjoram	½ teaspoon dried marjoram	
salt and pepper	salt and pepper	
		491
	Total	1034

Cook the noodles until tender. Meanwhile, chop the onion and celery and *sauté* them for 2-3 minutes in the oil in a saucepan. Slice the mushrooms, add them to the pan, and cook for a further 2-3 minutes. Sprinkle the flour into the saucepan, and stir. Slowly pour in the milk, stirring constantly, and bring to the boil. Stir in the chick peas (garbanzo beans), marjoram, and seasoning to taste. Combine the noodles with the bean mixture and transfer to a baking dish. Bake at 325°F (170°C/Gas Mark 3) for 25-30 minutes.

MENU 13

Breakfast

Imperial (Metric)	American	Calories
1 slice fresh pineapple	1 slice fresh pineapple	30
2 Shredded Wheat biscuits	2 Shredded Wheat biscuits	170
¼ pint (150ml) skimmed milk or 4 fl oz (100ml) soya milk	⅔ cup skim milk or ½ cup soymilk	50
2 teaspoons raw sugar	2 teaspoons raw sugar	35
		285

Lunch

MANHATTAN-STYLE CORN CHOWDER

Imperial (Metric)	American	Calories
4 oz (100g) tinned tomatoes	4 ounces canned tomatoes	12
2 sticks celery	2 stalks celery	10
1 small onion	1 small onion	12
4 oz (100g) potatoes	¼ pound potatoes	100
4 oz (100g) tinned sweetcorn	4 ounces canned corn	88
½ pint (¼ litre) water	1⅓ cups water	
salt and pepper to taste	salt and pepper to taste	
		222

Chop the tomatoes, celery, onion and potatoes. Put all ingredients in a saucepan and bring to the boil. Lower heat, cover pan, and simmer for about half an hour before serving.

Dinner

MIDDLE-EASTERN VEGETABLES WITH RICE

Imperial (Metric)	American	Calories
2 oz (50g) long-grain brown rice	⅓ cup long-grain brown rice	200
1 small onion	1 small onion	12
1 small carrot	1 small carrot	12
2 teaspoons vegetable margarine	2 teaspoons vegetable margarine	80
3 oz (75g) fresh or frozen green beans	3 ounces fresh or frozen green beans	21
1 oz (25g) almonds	¼ cup almonds	160
juice and grated rind of ½ lemon	juice and grated rind of ½ lemon	
½ teaspoon ground cinnamon	½ teaspoon ground cinnamon	
¼ teaspoon ground nutmeg	¼ teaspoon ground nutmeg	
salt and pepper, to taste	salt and pepper, to taste	
		485
	Total	992

Cook the rice until tender. Slice the onion and carrot thinly. *Sauté* them in the margarine 3-4 minutes. Slice the beans thinly and add them to the saucepan, along with the almonds, lemon rind and juice, cinnamon, nutmeg, salt and pepper. Cover the pan and simmer over a very low heat for about 20 minutes, stirring occasionally. Serve over the rice.

SUMMER MENUS

MENU 1

Breakfast

OAT AND SEED CEREAL

Imperial (Metric)	American	Calories
1½ oz (40g) rolled oats	⅓ cup rolled oats	160
1 oz (25g) sunflower seeds	¼ cup sunflower seeds	170
1 tablespoon clear honey	1 tablespoon honey	60
¼ pint (150ml) skimmed milk or 4 fl oz (100ml) soya milk	⅔ cup skim milk or ½ cup soymilk	50
1 oz (25g) raisins	⅙ cup raisins	70
4 oz (100g) strawberries	4 ounces strawberries	25
		535

Soak the oats in the milk for half an hour (or overnight). Mix in the sunflower seeds and raisins. Top with strawberries and sprinkle with honey.

Lunch

Imperial (Metric)	American	Calories
6 fl oz (175ml) tomato juice	¾ cup tomato juice	30
2 slices brown rye crispbread spread with a thin scraping of butter or vegetable margarine	2 slices brown rye crispbread spread with a thin scraping of butter or vegetable margarine	100
		130

Heat tomato juice gently and serve in a mug along with the brown rye crispbread.

Dinner

CHICK PEA (GARBANZO BEAN) AND VEGETABLE CASSEROLE

Imperial (Metric)	American	Calories
5 oz (125g) cooked chick peas	5 ounces cooked garbanzo beans	165
½ small cauliflower	½ small cauliflower	24
½ small green pepper	½ small green pepper	12
1 teaspoon Tamari (soya sauce)	1 teaspoon Tamari (soy sauce)	
½ teaspoon thyme	½ teaspoon thyme	
2 sticks celery	2 stalks celery	10
1 tablespoon wholemeal flour	1 tablespoon wholewheat flour	30
salt to taste	salt to taste	
Gravy:	Gravy:	
2 teaspoons vegetable oil	2 teaspoons vegetable oil	80
2 teaspoons wholemeal flour	2 teaspoons wholewheat flour	20
		341
	Total	1006

Chop vegetables finely. Steam them together in just enough water to cover bottom of saucepan until they are tender. Drain. Mash chick peas and vegetables together. Mix flour, Tamari, thyme and salt. Combine with chick pea and vegetable mixture. Spoon into oiled pan. Bake at 350°F (180°C/Gas Mark 4) for 30-40 minutes, until top is crusted over.

To make the gravy, heat the oil and add the flour. Stir well and slowly add just enough water to make a medium gravy. Add Tamari for taste, stirring constantly to avoid lumps.

MENU 2

<u>Breakfast</u>

FRUIT AND NUT BOWL

Imperial (Metric)	American	Calories
1½ oz (40g) ground almonds	⅓ cup ground almonds	240
dash almond essence	dash almond essence	
1 teaspoon vegetable oil	1 teaspoon vegetable oil	40
1 small banana	1 small banana	45
1 tablespoon honey	1 tablespoon honey	60
1-2 teaspoons lemon juice	1-2 teaspoons lemon juice	
1 apple	1 small apple	50
4 oz (100g) fresh raspberries	4 ounces raspberries	25
		460

Combine ground almonds, honey, oil, almond essence and lemon juice. Add enough water to make it a thick cream. Dice apples, slice bananas, mix with summer fruit and place in a bowl. Top with almond cream.

Lunch

CAULIFLOWER PÂTÉ

Imperial (Metric)	American	Calories
1 cauliflower ⎫ 1 clove garlic ⎭	1 cauliflower ⎫ 1 clove garlic ⎭	66
2 tablespoons lemon juice	2 tablespoons lemon juice	10
3 oz (75g) tahini (sesame paste)	⅓ cup tahini	510
½ teaspoon salt	½ teaspoon salt	
2 tablespoons water	2 tablespoons water	
		586
		÷ 3 = 195

3 slices rye crispbread
  (unbuttered)
	3 slices rye crispbread
	  (unbuttered)
		75

	(Crispbreads and pâté = 270)	

Cook and mash the cauliflower. Combine the tahini, crushed garlic, salt and lemon juice. Add water and stir till smooth. Add the mashed cauliflower and mix well. Divide into three equal portions; place ⅔ into a glass jar and keep in refrigerator. Serve the remaining third spread on the three slices of rye crispbread.

Dinner

STUFFED COURGETTES (ZUCCHINI)

Imperial (Metric)	American	Calories
2 large courgettes	2 large zucchini	50
3 fl oz (75ml) tomato juice	⅓ cup tomato juice	20
½ small onion ⎫ 1 small clove garlic ⎭	½ small onion ⎫ 1 small clove garlic ⎭	14
1 small slice wholemeal bread	1 small slice wholewheat bread	65
½ teaspoon marjoram or basil	½ teaspoon marjoram or basil	
1 oz (25g) wholemeal breadcrumbs	½ cup fresh wholewheat breadcrumbs	65
salt to taste	salt to taste	
3 oz (75g) small new potatoes	3 ounces small potatoes	75
		289
	Total	1019

Steam the courgettes (zucchini) in their skins for 10 minutes. Cut them lengthwise and scoop out the centres, saving the pulp. Chop the onion and crush the garlic. Soak the bread in the tomato juice. Mash it and add the courgette (zucchini) pulp, garlic and onion, half the breadcrumbs, salt and herbs, mixing well. Stuff the shells with this mixture. Sprinkle with the rest of the crumbs. Bake for 30-45 minutes at 350°F (180°C/Gas Mark 4). Serve with the cooked potatoes.

MENU 3

Breakfast

Imperial (Metric)	American	Calories
4 fl oz (100ml) unsweetened orange juice	½ cup orange juice	40
2 oz (50g) Shredded Wheat or Weetabix served with:	2 ounces Shredded Wheat or wheat flakes served with:	200
¼ pint (150ml) skimmed milk or 4 fl oz (100ml) soya milk	⅔ cup skim milk or ½ cup soymilk	50
1 tablespoon brown sugar	1 tablespoon brown sugar	50
		340

Lunch

NUT SAVOURY SALAD

Imperial (Metric)	American	Calories
1 oz (25g) wholemeal breadcrumbs	½ cup fresh wholewheat breadcrumbs	65
1 small spring onion }	1 small scallion }	15
1 small tomato	1 small tomato	
Fresh or dried chopped mint or parsley	Fresh or dried mint or parsley	
1 oz (25g) almonds	¼ cup almonds	160
mixed salad ingredients	mixed salad ingredients	20
		260

Peel the tomato and chop it finely. Chop spring onion (scallion). Put in a mixing bowl. Grind almonds finely. Add breadcrumbs, herbs and nuts to mixing bowl. Mix well together. Press down in a small bowl, put something on top of the mixture to weigh it down, and leave for at least 2 hours. Serve with a salad of lettuce, carrots, watercress and raw mushrooms.

Dinner

BLACK-EYED BEANS (PEAS) AND NUTS

Imperial (Metric)	American	Calories
2 oz (50g) black-eyed beans	¼ cup black-eyed peas	170
1 small onion	1 small onion	12
2 teaspoons vegetable oil	2 teaspoons vegetable oil	80
salt to taste	salt to taste	
1 tablespoon tomato purée	1 tablespoon tomato paste	10
½ oz (15g) almonds	⅛ cup almonds	80
2 tablespoons water	2 tablespoons water	
1 tablespoon minced parsley	1 tablespoon minced parsley	
1 small slice unbuttered wholemeal bread	1 small slice unbuttered wholewheat bread	65
		417
	Total	1017

Soak beans overnight and cook until tender (about 45 minutes), adding salt only near the end. Drain. Chop onion and *sauté* in oil until soft. Add beans, tomato *purée*, nuts and water. Simmer for 10 minutes longer. Serve topped with parsley, accompanied by bread.

MENU 4

Breakfast

Imperial (Metric)	American	Calories
4 fl oz (100ml) unsweetened grapefruit juice	½ cup grapefruit juice	35
1 poached egg or 3 oz (75g) firm tofu, thinly sliced and grilled on each side, served with 1 slice thinly buttered wholemeal toast	1 poached egg or 3 ounces firm tofu, thinly sliced and broiled on each side, served with 1 slice thinly buttered wholewheat toast	190
1 small tomato, grilled	2½ ounces tomato slices, broiled	10
		235

Lunch

CAULIFLOWER PÂTÉ

Imperial (Metric)	American	Calories
Use ⅓ of the remaining pâté from Summer Menu 2	Use ⅓ of the remaining pâté from Summer Menu 2	195
3 slices rye crispbread (unbuttered)	3 slices rye crispbread (unbuttered)	75
		270

Dinner

SAVOURY SUNFLOWER SEEDS

Imperial (Metric)	American	Calories
2 oz (50g) brown rice	1/3 cup brown rice	200
1 small onion	1 small onion	12
2 teaspoons vegetable oil	2 teaspoons vegetable oil	80
4 sticks celery	4 stalks celery	20
1 oz (25g) sunflower seeds	1/4 cup sunflower seeds	170
2 oz (50g) mushrooms	1 cup mushrooms	5
1 tablespoon parsley	1 tablespoon parsley	
1/2 teaspoon powdered ginger	1/2 teaspoon powdered ginger	
		487
	Total	992

Cook the rice. Chop the onions and mushrooms and *sauté* in oil. Add the celery, parsley and ginger. Cover and cook for 10 minutes over low heat. Add seeds and serve over the rice.

MENU 5

Breakfast

Imperial (Metric)	American	Calories
2 oz (50g) muesli	½ cup muesli	220
served with:	served with:	
¼ pint (150ml) skimmed milk or 4 fl oz (100ml) soya milk	⅔ cup skim milk or ½ cup soymilk	50
4 oz (100g) strawberries or raspberries	4 ounces strawberries or raspberries	25
		295

Lunch

QUICK NUTTY NOSH

Imperial (Metric)	American	Calories
1 oz (25g) finely ground cashew nuts	¼ cup finely ground cashews	180
1 oz (25g) finely ground Brazil nuts	¼ cup finely ground Brazil nuts	180
½ teaspoon yeast extract (or more to taste)	½ teaspoon yeast extract (or more to taste)	5
salad of lettuce, tomato, cucumber and spring onion	salad of lettuce, tomato, cucumber and scallion	15
		380

Combine nuts and yeast extract and mould with your hands into small balls, and place on top of the salad.

Dinner

WHEAT AND VEGETABLES

Imperial (Metric)	American	Calories
2 teaspoons vegetable oil	2 teaspoons vegetable oil	80
1 small onion	1 small onion	12
2 oz (50g) wheat berries (whole wheat grains)	½ cup wheat berries (whole wheat grains)	200
1 bunch watercress	1 bunch watercress	5
1 small carrot	1 small carrot	10
1 small clove garlic	1 small clove garlic	
1 tablespoon Tamari (soya sauce) }	1 tablespoon Tamari (soy sauce) }	5
2 tablespoons water	2 tablespoons water	
		312
	Total	987

Cover the wheat berries with boiling water in the morning and leave to soak. In the evening cook them in fresh water until tender (about 25 minutes). Chop the onion and watercress, dice the carrots and crush the garlic. *Sauté* the onion in the oil for 3-4 minutes, then add the rest of the vegetables and stir well for 5 minutes. Add the cooked wheat berries and mix with vegetables. Continue to stir for another 3 minutes. Add the water and Tamari, cover, and simmer for 5 minutes longer.

MENU 6

Breakfast

NUTTY BANANA CEREAL

Imperial (Metric)	American	Calories
1 oz (25g) rolled oats	¼ cup rolled oats	105
1 small banana	1 small banana	45
½ oz (15g) sesame seeds	⅛ cup sesame seeds	80
½ oz (15g) raisins	½ ounce raisins	35
½ oz (15g) almonds	⅛ cup almonds	80
½ oz (15g) cashews	⅛ cup cashews	90
¼ pint (150ml) skimmed milk or 4 fl oz (100ml) soya milk	⅔ cup skim milk or ½ cup soymilk	50
		485

Slice banana. Cut almonds and cashews in half. Mix dry
ingredients together and top with milk.

Lunch

CAULIFLOWER PÂTÉ

Imperial (Metric)	American	Calories
Use the remaining portion of the pâté from Summer Menu 2	Use the remaining portion of the pâté from Summer Menu 2	195
3 slices rye crispbread (unbuttered)	3 slices rye crispbread (unbuttered)	75
		270

Dinner

VEGETABLE CASSEROLE

Imperial (Metric)	American	Calories
1 small onion	1 small onion	
1 small clove garlic	1 small clove garlic	14
2 small tomatoes	2 small tomatoes	20
2 small courgettes	2 small zucchini	24
1 small leek	1 small leek	20
1 small green pepper	1 small green pepper	24
2 oz (50g) mushrooms	1 cup mushrooms	5
2 teaspoons lemon juice	2 teaspoons lemon juice	
1 tablespoon vegetable oil	1 tablespoon vegetable oil	120
1 tablespoon tomato purée	1 tablespoon tomato paste	10
1 teaspoon dried mixed herbs	1 teaspoon dried mixed herbs	
salt and pepper to taste	salt and pepper to taste	
		237
	Total	992

Chop onion. Chop or crush garlic. Skin tomatoes, then slice them.
Wash and slice courgettes (zucchini), mushrooms, green pepper
(discarding seeds) and leek. Mix *purée* (paste) with lemon juice. Stir
in herbs. Fry onion, garlic and leek in the oil until golden. Put all
the vegetables in a casserole dish. Pour in tomato mixture. Season.
Cover dish with lid or foil. Cook in centre of 375°F (190°C/Gas
Mark 5) oven for 1 hour or until leek and pepper are tender.

MENU 7

Breakfast

Imperial (Metric)	American	Calories
¼ pint (150ml) orange juice	⅔ cup orange juice	50
2 oz (50g) Fru-grains	½ cup wholegrain cereal	195
served with:	served with:	
¼ pint (150ml) skimmed milk or 4 fl oz (100ml) soya milk	⅔ cup skim milk or ½ cup soymilk	50
		295

Lunch

MIXED SALAD

Imperial (Metric)	American	Calories
Mixed salad ingredients (lettuce, tomato, grated carrot, radish, cucumber)	Mixed salad ingredients (lettuce, tomato, carrot, radish, cucumber)	20
topped with:	topped with:	
1 oz (25g) finely ground almonds (roasted first if desired)	¼ cup finely ground almonds (roasted first if desired)	160
		180

Dinner

STUFFED CABBAGE LEAVES

Imperial (Metric)	American	Calories
2 oz (50g) brown rice	⅓ cup brown rice	200
1 small onion	1 small onion	12
1 tablespoon raisins	1 tablespoon raisins	25
1 oz (25g) sunflower seeds	¼ cup sunflower seeds	170
1 teaspoon arrowroot powder	1 teaspoon arrowroot powder	10
about half a dozen spring cabbage leaves	about half a dozen cabbage leaves	10
salt to taste	salt to taste	
2 teaspoons vegetable oil	2 teaspoons vegetable oil	80
1 teaspoon caraway seeds	1 teaspoon caraway seeds	
4 fl oz (100ml) tomato juice	½ cup tomato juice	24
½ teaspoon basil or marjoram	½ teaspoon sweet basil or marjoram	
		531
	Total	1006

Cover rice with boiling water and soak for several hours. Cook in fresh, salted water until tender, approximately 20 minutes. Chop onion and *sauté* in oil until tender. Combine rice, onion, sunflower and caraway seeds and raisins. Steam cabbage leaves for a few minutes until tenderized. Place a small amount of rice mixture in centre of each leaf and roll up. Place in a casserole dish or on a baking tray. Heat tomato juice with basil or marjoram, leaving a small amount to mix with arrowroot. When juice is boiling add arrowroot mixture and stir over medium heat until thickened. Pour over cabbage leaves. Bake in moderate oven 350°F (180°C/Gas Mark 4) for 15-20 minutes.

MENU 8

Breakfast

Imperial (Metric)	American	Calories
¼ pint (150ml) orange juice	⅔ cup orange juice	50
scrambled egg made with 1 large egg and a few drops skimmed milk; or scrambled tofu, made by mashing 3 oz (75g) tofu with 1 teaspoon soya sauce and pinch turmeric	scrambled egg made with 1 large egg and a few drops skim milk; or scrambled tofu, made by mashing 3 ounces tofu with 1 teaspoon soy sauce and pinch turmeric	95
1½ teaspoons vegetable margarine	1½ teaspoons vegetable margarine	60
1 slice wholemeal bread	1 slice wholewheat bread	75
		280

Lunch

TAHINI SPREAD

Imperial (Metric)	American	Calories
1 oz (25g) tahini	½ cup tahini	170
3 slices brown rye crispbread	3 slices brown rye crispbread	75
1 teaspoon Tamari (soya sauce)	1 teaspoon Tamari (soy sauce)	
1 small carrot	1 small carrot	10
water as required	water as required	
		255

Combine tahini with Tamari and add just enough water to make it a firm spreading consistency (water thickens the mixture). Spread on crispbread. Eat with 1 raw carrot.

Dinner

SUMMER STEW

Imperial (Metric)	American	Calories
1 small onion	1 small onion	12
1 small leek	1 small leek	20
4 oz (100g) spinach leaves	4 ounces spinach leaves	15
2 oz (50g) red lentils	⅓ cup red lentils	150
1 small carrot	1 small carrot	10
2 teaspoons vegetable oil	2 teaspoons vegetable oil	80
¾ oz (20g) rolled oats	2 tablespoons rolled oats	75
4 oz (100g) new potatoes	4 ounces small potatoes	100
		462
	Total	997

Chop onion and leek and fry for 2-3 minutes in hot oil. Add sliced carrot and *sauté* vegetables 2-3 minutes longer. Add lentils and enough water to cover them. Wash and chop spinach and add to mixture. Simmer until all cooked (about 20 minutes) then add the oats to thicken the mixture and stir until it is nice and creamy. Serve with boiled potatoes.

MENU 9

Breakfast

Imperial (Metric)	American	Calories
2 oz (50g) muesli	½ cup muesli	220
served with:	served with:	
¼ pint (150ml) skimmed milk or 4 fl oz (100ml) soya milk	⅔ cup skim milk or ½ cup soymilk	50
1 large ripe peach	1 large ripe peach	50
		320

Lunch

Imperial (Metric)	American	Calories
mixed salad ingredients (lettuce, tomato, cucumber, radish, spring onion, grated carrot)	mixed salad ingredients (lettuce, tomato, cucumber, radish, scallion, grated carrot)	20
topped with:	topped with:	
4 oz (100g) sliced smoked tofu, either plain or lightly grilled	4 ounces sliced smoked tofu, either plain or lightly broiled	116
		136

Dinner

CHICK PEAS (GARBANZO BEANS) IN SPANISH SAUCE

Imperial (Metric)	American	Calories
2 oz (50g) brown rice	⅓ cup brown rice	200
6 oz (150g) cooked chick peas	6 ounces cooked garbanzo beans	198
1 small green pepper	1 small green pepper	24
1 small onion ⎫ 1 small clove garlic ⎭	1 small onion ⎫ 1 small clove garlic ⎭	14
pinch cayenne pepper	pinch cayenne	
salt to taste	salt to taste	
2 teaspoons vegetable oil	2 teaspoons vegetable oil	80
1 tablespoon chopped parsley	1 tablespoon chopped parsley	
4 oz (100g) tomatoes	4 ounces tomatoes	16
		532
	Total	988

Cook the rice. Chop the onion, green pepper and garlic and fry in oil until tender. Chop and add parsley, tomatoes and seasoning. Cook on low heat for 20-30 minutes. Add cooked chick peas (garbanzo beans). Serve over the rice.

MENU 10

Breakfast

Imperial (Metric)	American	Calories
2 oz (50g) muesli	½ cup muesli	220
2 small sliced plums	2 small sliced plums	50
¼ pint (150ml) skimmed milk or 4 fl oz (100ml) soya milk	⅔ cup skim milk or ½ cup soymilk	50
		320

Lunch

CREAM OF VEGETABLE SOUP

Imperial (Metric)	American	Calories
1 small carrot	1 small carrot	10
4 oz (100g) potatoes	4 ounces potatoes	100
1 stick celery	1 stalk celery	5
1 small onion	1 small onion	12
1 sprig parsley	1 sprig parsley	
¼ pint (150ml) water	⅔ cup water	
¼ pint (150ml) skimmed milk or 4 fl oz (100ml) soya milk	⅔ cup skim milk or ½ cup soymilk	50
salt and pepper to taste	salt and pepper to taste	
2 unbuttered brown rye crispbreads	2 unbuttered brown rye crispbreads	50
		227

Chop the carrot, potatoes, celery and onion finely. Put them in a saucepan, along with the parsley and the water. Bring to the boil, then lower heat, cover pan, and simmer for about 15 minutes, by which time the vegetables should be soft. Cool briefly. Pour the vegetable mixture into a liquidizer, along with the milk, and blend thoroughly. Return the soup to the saucepan, re-heat gently and season to taste. Serve accompanied by the crispbread.

Dinner

TOFU-STUFFED AUBERGINE (EGGPLANT)

Imperial (Metric)	American	Calories
½ lb (¼ kilo) aubergine	½ pound eggplant	30
1 small onion }	1 small onion }	
1 small clove garlic }	1 small clove garlic }	14
2 teaspoons vegetable margarine	2 teaspoons vegetable margarine	80
4 oz (100g) tofu	½ cup tofu	116
1½ oz (60g) fresh wholemeal breadcrumbs	¼ cup fresh wholewheat breadcrumbs	100
½ oz (15g) sunflower seeds	⅛ cup sunflower seeds	85
½ teaspoon dried basil	½ teaspoon sweet basil	
1-2 teaspoons Tamari (soya sauce)	1-2 teaspoons Tamari (soy sauce)	
2 teaspoons Parmesan cheese or nutritional yeast	2 teaspoons Parmesan cheese or nutritional yeast	25
4 oz (100g) green beans	¼ pound green beans	20
		470
	Total	1017

Cook the rice. Chop the top off the aubergine (eggplant) and halve it lengthwise. Put the halves, skin side up, into a saucepan, cover with 2-3 inches of boiling water, cover and simmer for 10-15 minutes until soft. Chop the onion and garlic finely and *sauté* in the margarine until beginning to brown. Remove from heat and crumble in the tofu. Add the breadcrumbs, sunflower seeds, basil and Tamari. When the cooked aubergine (eggplant) halves are cool enough to handle, gently remove the flesh from the skins. Place the skins into an oven dish. Chop the flesh, add to the tofu mixture. Mix thoroughly. Pile the mixture onto the skins. Sprinkle a teaspoon of cheese or yeast on top of each. Bake at 375°F (190°C/ Gas Mark 5) for about half an hour. Serve with lightly-steamed green beans.

MENU 11

Breakfast

Imperial (Metric)	American	Calories
2 oz (100g) wheatflakes served with:	2 ounces wheatflakes served with:	200
¼ pint (150ml) skimmed milk or 4 fl oz (150ml) soya milk	⅔ cup skim milk or ½ cup soymilk	50
2 teaspoons raw sugar	2 teaspoons raw sugar	34
1 sliced peach	1 sliced peach	50
		334

Lunch

CHILLED SUMMER SOUP

Imperial (Metric)	American	Calories
3 oz (75g) dairy or soya yogurt	⅓ cup dairy or soy yogurt	45
1½ teaspoons vegetable oil	1½ teaspoons vegetable oil	60
5 oz (125g) tinned tomatoes (with juice)	5 ounces canned tomatoes (with juice)	15
½ teaspoon lemon juice	½ teaspoon lemon juice	
¼ teaspoon marjoram	¼ teaspoon marjoram	
Freshly ground black pepper	Freshly ground black pepper	
1 unbuttered brown rye crispbread	1 unbuttered brown rye crispbread	25
		145

Place all the ingredients (except the crispbread) in a liquidizer and blend thoroughly. Chill in the refrigerator (or chill the ingredients before using and serve immediately), accompanied by the crispbread.

Dinner

PASTA E FAGIOLI

Imperial (Metric)	American	Calories
1 small onion	1 small onion	12
1 small carrot	1 small carrot	10
½ small green pepper	½ small green pepper	8
2 teaspoons olive oil	2 teaspoons olive oil	80
2 oz (50g) smoked tofu	2 ounces smoked tofu	58
4 oz (100g) tinned tomatoes	4 ounces canned tomatoes	12
⅓ pint (200ml) water	¾ cup water	
1 small bay leaf	1 small bay leaf	
½ teaspoon basil	½ teaspoon sweet basil	
½ teaspoon oregano	½ teaspoon oregano	
1½ oz (40g) red lentils	¼ cup red lentils	120
2½ oz (65g) wholemeal spaghetti	2½ ounces wholewheat spaghetti	250
		550
	Total	1029

Chop the onion, carrot and green pepper quite finely. *Sauté* in a medium-sized saucepan in the oil for 2-3 minutes. Dice the tofu finely. Add it to the saucepan and *sauté* a further 2-3 minutes over a fairly high heat, stirring often. Chop the tomatoes coarsely. Add to the saucepan, along with the water, and bring to the boil. Stir in the herbs and the lentils. Lower heat, cover pan and simmer for 20-25 minutes, stirring occasionally (if it appears to be drying out then add a little more water). Meanwhile, cook the spaghetti until just tender. Drain it well, and mix it with the lentils and vegetables. Cook for a minute or two longer and serve.

MENU 12

Breakfast

Imperial (Metric)	American	Calories
1 nectarine	1 nectarine	50

OATCAKES WITH SWEET ALMOND SPREAD

Imperial (Metric)	American	Calories
2 tablespoons ground almonds	2 tablespoons ground almonds	60
2 teaspoons honey	2 teaspoons honey	40
½ teaspoon vegetable oil	½ teaspoon vegetable oil	20
few drops almond essence	few drops almond essence	
water as required	water as required	
3 oatcakes	3 oatcakes	180
		350

In a small bowl mix together the ground almonds, honey, oil and almond essence. Add a few drops of water, just enough to make the mixture into a spreadable consistency. Spread onto oatcakes.

Lunch

SPINACH AND RED PEPPER SALAD

Imperial (Metric)	American	Calories
3 oz (75g) fresh spinach	3 ounces fresh spinach	12
½ small red pepper	½ small red pepper	16
3 oz (75g) dairy or soya yogurt	⅓ cup dairy or soy yogurt	45
½ teaspoon garlic salt	½ teaspoon garlic salt	
freshly ground black pepper	freshly ground black pepper	
1 tablespoon Smokey Snaps	1 tablespoon imitation bacon bits	58
2 unbuttered brown rye crispbreads	2 unbuttered brown rye crispbreads	50
		181

Wash the spinach thoroughly, dry it (a salad spinner is very useful for this), and shred it coarsely. Slice the pepper into thin strips. Mix together the yogurt, garlic salt and pepper. Pour over the spinach and red pepper and mix thoroughly. Sprinkle with the Smokey Snaps (imitation bacon bits) and serve immediately, accompanied by the crispbread.

Dinner

BEAN AND VEGETABLE MIX WITH BULGUR

Imperial (Metric)	American	Calories
2 oz (50g) bulgur wheat	½ cup bulgur wheat	200
1 small onion	1 small onion	12
2 teaspoons vegetable oil	2 teaspoons vegetable oil	80
2 oz (50g) mushrooms	1 cup mushrooms	5
2 sticks celery	2 stalks celery	10
1 small courgette	1 small zucchini	12
6 oz (150g) cooked borlotti beans	6 ounces cooked pinto beans	156
1 teaspoon Tamari (soya sauce)	1 teaspoon Tamari (soy sauce)	
1 tablespoon vegetable stock	1 tablespoon vegetable stock	
1 tablespoon tomato purée	1 tablespoon tomato paste	10
½ teaspoon marjoram	½ teaspoon marjoram	
freshly ground black pepper	freshly ground black pepper	
few drops Tabasco sauce (optional)	few drops Tabasco sauce (optional)	
		485
	Total	1016

Cover the bulgur wheat with about three times its volume in lightly salted water, bring to the boil, lower heat, and simmer until the water has been absorbed, about 10 minutes. Meanwhile, chop the onion and *sauté* it in the oil in a wok or saucepan for 2-3 minutes. Chop the mushrooms, celery and courgettes (zucchini) quite finely, and add to the onion. Stir-fry for a minute or two, then add the beans, Tamari, stock, tomato *purée* (paste), marjoram, pepper and Tabasco sauce (if used). Stir well, then lower heat, cover wok or pan, and simmer for about 5 minutes. Serve the bean mixture over the bulgur wheat.

MENU 13

Breakfast

Imperial (Metric)	American	Calories
1½ oz (40g) Granola-type cereal	1½ ounces Granola	200
4 oz (100g) fresh strawberries	4 ounces fresh strawberries	25
¼ pint (150ml) skimmed milk or 4 fl oz (100ml) soya milk	⅔ cup skim milk or ½ cup soymilk	50
		275

Lunch

MIXED BEAN AND PEA SALAD

Imperial (Metric)	American	Calories
4 oz (100g) fresh green beans	4 ounces fresh green beans	16
4 oz (100g) fresh peas (after hulling)	4 ounces fresh peas (after hulling)	60
2 teaspoons olive oil	2 teaspoons olive oil	80
1 teaspoon cider vinegar	1 teaspoon cider vinegar	
½ teaspoon garlic salt	½ teaspoon garlic salt	
black pepper to taste	black pepper to taste	
1 tablespoon chopped parsley	1 tablespoon chopped parsley	
4 oz (100g) cooked borlotti beans	4 ounces cooked pinto beans	102
2 slices unbuttered brown rye crispbread	2 slices unbuttered brown rye crispbread	50
		308

Slice the green beans (either lengthwise or crosswise, depending on size of bean and personal preference) and cook until just tender. Cook the peas until tender. Drain and cool both. In a small bowl or cup mix together the oil, vinegar, garlic salt, pepper and parsley. Drain the borlotti (pinto) beans and put them in a bowl. Add the peas and green beans. Spoon the dressing over them and mix thoroughly. Chill before serving, accompanied by the crispbread.

Dinner

BAKED PASTA

Imperial (Metric)	American	Calories
2½ oz (65g) wholemeal macaroni or shells	2½ ounces wholewheat macaroni or shells	250
1 small onion 1 small clove garlic }	1 small onion 1 small clove garlic }	14
2 teaspoons olive oil	2 teaspoons olive oil	80
4 oz (100g) tomatoes	4 ounces tomatoes	16
1 small courgette	1 small zucchini	12
1½ tablespoons vegetable stock	1½ tablespoons vegetable stock	
½ teaspoon oregano	½ teaspoon oregano	
½ teaspoon basil	½ teaspoon sweet basil	
salt and pepper	salt and pepper	
2 teaspoons Parmesan cheese or nutritional yeast	2 teaspoons Parmesan cheese or nutritional yeast	25
1 teaspoon butter or vegetable margarine	1 teaspoon butter or vegetable margarine	40
		437
	Total	1020

Put the pasta on to cook. Chop the onion and garlic. *Sauté* them in the oil until just beginning to brown. Skin and chop the tomatoes. Dice the courgette (zucchini). Add them to the saucepan, along with the stock, herbs and seasoning. Lower heat, cover saucepan and simmer for 4-5 minutes, until the courgette (zucchini) is crisp-tender. When the pasta is just tender, drain it and mix with the above. Turn the mixture into a baking dish. Sprinkle with the cheese or yeast and dot with the butter or margarine. Bake at 375°F (190°C/Gas Mark 5) for about 20 minutes. Serve immediately.

AUTUMN MENUS

MENU 1

<u>Breakfast</u>

HIGH PROTEIN CEREAL

Imperial (Metric)	American	Calories
1 oz (25g) wheat germ	¼ cup wheat germ	100
½ oz (15g) sunflower seeds	⅛ cup sunflower seeds	85
1 apple	1 small apple	50
½ oz (15g) sesame seeds	⅛ cup sesame seeds	80
¼ pint (150ml) skimmed milk or 4 fl oz (100ml) soya milk	⅔ cup skim milk or ½ cup soymilk	50
1 oz (25g) chopped dates	⅛ cup chopped dates	70
		435

Grind seeds in a blender, combine with wheat germ in a bowl. Add milk. Top with chopped apple and dates.

Lunch

JERUSALEM ARTICHOKE SOUP

Imperial (Metric)	American	Calories
4 oz (100g) Jerusalem artichokes	4 ounces Jerusalem artichokes	25
1 teaspoon vegetable margarine	1 teaspoon vegetable margarine	35
¼ pint (150ml) skimmed milk or 4 fl oz (100ml) soya milk	⅔ cup skim milk or ½ cup soymilk	50
1 small onion	1 small onion	12
seasoning to taste	seasoning to taste	
1 slice unbuttered rye crispbread	1 slice unbuttered rye crispbread	25
		147

Scrub artichokes (it is not necessary to peel them) and chop. Chop onion and brown in margarine. Combine all ingredients and simmer gently until artichokes are tender. Pour into liquidizer and liquidize thoroughly. Reheat gently.

Dinner

STUFFED MARROW (SUMMER SQUASH)

Imperial (Metric)	American	Calories
½ lb (225g) marrow section	½ pound summer squash	30
1 oz (25g) almonds	¼ cup almonds	160
1 small onion	1 small onion	12
1 small tomato	1 small tomato	12
¼ pint (150ml) tomato juice	⅔ cup tomato juice	30
1 teaspoon basil	1 teaspoon sweet basil	
1 oz (25g) fresh breadcrumbs	½ cup fresh breadcrumbs	65
2 teaspoons vegetable oil	2 teaspoons vegetable oil	80
2 oz (50g) mushrooms	1 cup mushrooms	5
salt and pepper to taste	salt and pepper to taste	
1 heaped teaspoon arrowroot	1 heaped teaspoon arrowroot	20
		414
	Total	996

Parboil the marrow (squash) whole for a few minutes, then cut it in half lengthwise and scoop out and set aside the flesh and seeds. Mince the onion and mushrooms and fry in the oil until tender. Grind the nuts, mix with the breadcrumbs and place under the grill (broiler), turning frequently, until toasted. Combine the breadcrumb mixture and mushroom mixture with the chopped marrow (squash) flesh (including the seeds if the marrow (squash) is young and tender) and the tomato which has been skinned and chopped. Add seasoning to taste. Place in the narrow cavity of the marrow (squash). Bake in a moderate oven at at 350°F (180°C/Gas Mark 4) for 30 minutes. Serve with sauce made from tomato juice which has been heated with the basil and thickened with arrowroot dissolved in a little cold water.

MENU 2

Breakfast

Imperial (Metric)	American	Calories
¼ pint (150ml) grapefruit juice	⅔ cup grapefruit juice	45
1 poached egg or 3 oz (75g) firm tofu, thinly sliced and grilled on each side	1 poached egg or 3 ounces firm tofu, thinly sliced and broiled on each side	90
1 small tomato, grilled	2½ ounces tomato slices, broiled	10
2 oz (50g) grilled mushrooms	1 cup broiled mushrooms	5
1 slice lightly buttered wholemeal toast	1 slice lightly buttered wholewheat toast	100
		250

Lunch

NUT MOULD

Imperial (Metric)	American	Calories
1 Shredded Wheat biscuit	1 Shredded Wheat biscuit	85
1 oz (25g) almonds	¼ cup almonds	160
1 oz (25g) walnuts	¼ cup walnuts	150
1 teaspoon tomato purée (or more if required)	1 teaspoon tomato paste (or more if required)	4
Mixed salad ingredients (lettuce, tomato, grated carrot, chopped green pepper, chopped raw mushrooms, spring onion)	Mixed salad ingredients (lettuce, tomato, grated carrot, chopped green pepper, chopped raw mushrooms, scallions)	20
dried mixed herbs, to taste	dried mixed herbs, to taste	
		419

Grind nuts. Crumble Shredded Wheat. Combine with tomato *purée* (paste) and herbs. Press into a small bowl and leave in a cool place until required. Turn out and serve with salad.

Dinner

PEANUT PILAU

Imperial (Metric)	American	Calories
2 oz (50g) brown rice	⅓ cup brown rice	200
1 small onion	1 small onion	12
1 tomato	1 small tomato	12
½ small green pepper	½ small green pepper	12
½ teaspoon mixed herbs	½ teaspoon mixed herbs	
1 teaspoon vegetable margarine	1 teaspoon vegetable margarine	40
2 oz (50g) mushrooms	1 cup mushrooms	5
2 sticks celery	2 stalks celery	5
½ teaspoon yeast extract	½ teaspoon yeast extract	5
½ oz (15g) roasted peanuts (if using salted variety rinse under tap to get rid of excess oil and salt)	⅛ cup roasted peanuts (if using salted variety rinse under tap to get rid of excess oil and salt)	85
		376
	Total	1045

Cover rice with boiling water and soak overnight. Skin tomato and chop together with onion, celery, mushrooms and green pepper and fry in margarine for 3-5 minutes. Drain rice and add to the pan along with yeast extract and herbs. Cover with water and bring to the boil. Simmer until tender (20-25 minutes). Add peanuts and mix in well.

MENU 3

Breakfast

Imperial (Metric)	American	Calories
¼ pint (150ml) grapefruit juice (unsweetened)	⅔ cup unsweetened grapefruit juice	50

OATMEAL PORRIDGE

Imperial (Metric)	American	Calories
2 oz (50g) medium oatmeal (much more satisfying than oatflakes)	½ cup medium oatmeal (much more satisfying than oatflakes)	200
salt and water, to taste (depending on how thick or thin the porridge is preferred)	salt and water, to taste (depending on how thick or thin the porridge is preferred)	
2 fl oz (50ml) skimmed milk or 1½ fl oz (35ml) soya milk	¼ cup skim milk or ⅙ cup soymilk	25
2 teaspoons brown sugar	2 teaspoons brown sugar	34
		309

Pour oatmeal into about 3 times its volume in water (the exact amount will depend on whether one prefers a thin or thick porridge). Bring the oatmeal and water to the boil and add salt to taste. Lower heat and simmer uncovered for 5-10 minutes. Serve topped with the milk and sugar.

Lunch

BAKED BEANS ON TOAST

Imperial (Metric)	American	Calories
5 oz (150g) tinned baked beans	5 ounces canned vegetarian baked beans	125
1 slice lightly buttered wholemeal toast	1 slice lightly buttered wholwheat toast	100
		225

Serve baked beans over the slice of lightly buttered toast.

Dinner

CHOP SUEY

Imperial (Metric)	American	Calories
2 oz (50g) short-grain brown rice	⅓ cup brown rice	200
½ oz (15g) almonds	⅛ cup almonds	80
2 sticks celery	2 stalks celery	5
2 oz (50g) white cabbage	2 ounces white cabbage	15
1 heaped teaspoon arrowroot powder	1 heaped teaspoon arrowroot powder	30
⅛ pint (70ml) cold water	⅓ cup cold water	
4 oz (100g) mung bean sprouts	4 ounces mung bean sprouts	25
1 small onion ⎫	1 small onion ⎫	
1 small clove garlic ⎭	1 small clove garlic ⎭	14
4 oz (100g) mushrooms	2 cups mushrooms	10
1 tablespoon Tamari (soya sauce)	1 tablespoon Tamari (soy sauce)	
2 teaspoons vegetable oil	2 teaspoons vegetable oil	80
		459
	Total	993

Cook the rice. Toast the almonds lightly under the grill (broiler).
Slice onion, celery and mushrooms. Crush garlic. Shred cabbage.
Fry all of these ingredients in the oil for 5 minutes. Dissolve the
arrowroot in the water and mix in the Tamari. Add this to the
frying pan, stir in the mixture well as it thickens and simmer for
3 minutes. Add the almonds and then the bean sprouts, stirring
well until they are slightly wilted. Serve over the cooked rice, with
additional Tamari if desired.

MENU 4

Breakfast

Imperial (Metric)	American	Calories
2 oz (50g) Granola-type cereal	½ cup Granola-type cereal	270
topped with:	topped with:	
¼ pint (150ml) skimmed milk or 4 fl oz (100ml) soya milk	⅔ cup skim milk or ½ cup soymilk	50
1 small orange, segmented	1 small orange, segmented	40
		360

Lunch

Imperial (Metric)	American	Calories
6 fl oz (175ml) tinned mixed vegetable juice	¾ cup canned mixed vegetable juice	35
2 slices brown rye crispbread, thinly spread with butter or vegetable margarine	2 slices brown rye crispbread, thinly spread with butter or vegetable margarine	100
		135

Heat vegetable juice and serve in a mug, accompanied by brown rye crispbread.

Dinner

LENTIL MUSHROOM STEW

Imperial (Metric)	American	Calories
2 oz (50g) brown or green lentils	⅓ cup brown or green lentils	160
vegetable stock as required	vegetable stock as required	
1 small carrot	1 small carrot	5
4 oz (100g) tinned tomatoes	4 ounces canned tomatoes	12
2 teaspoons vegetable oil	2 teaspoons vegetable oil	80
2 oz (50g) short-grain brown rice	⅓ cup brown rice	200
1 teaspoon basil	1 teaspoon sweet basil	
1 stick celery	1 stalk celery	5
1 small onion	1 small onion	12
2 oz (50g) mushrooms	1 cup mushrooms	5
1 tablespoon cider vinegar	1 tablespoon cider vinegar	
		479
	Total	974

Soak rice and lentils overnight. Put rice on to cook. Add enough vegetable stock to lentils to cover them. Chop onion and mushrooms, fry briefly in oil. Chop celery and carrots finely, add to mushrooms, *sauté* 2-3 minutes longer. Add vegetables to lentils along with tomatoes and basil, and cook until lentils are tender (25-30 minutes). Add vinegar just before serving over brown rice.

MENU 5

Breakfast

Imperial (Metric)	American	Calories
4 fl oz (100ml) unsweetened pineapple juice	½ cup unsweetened pineapple juice	60

MILLET PORRIDGE

Imperial (Metric)	American	Calories
1½ oz (40g) millet	¼ cup millet	150
pinch of salt	pinch of salt	
water	water	
⅛ pint (70ml) skimmed milk or 2 fl oz (50ml) soya milk	⅓ cup skim milk or ¼ cup soymilk	25
¾ oz (20g) honey	1½ tablespoons honey	60
		295

Cook millet with salt and water (approximately 3 times volume of the cereal) for 10-20 minutes. Top with skimmed milk and honey.

Lunch

WINTER SALAD

Imperial (Metric)	American	Calories
2 oz (50g) turnip or swede	2 ounces turnip or rutabaga	12
2 oz (50g) white cabbage	2 ounces white cabbage	12
1 small carrot	1 small carrot	5
1 small apple	1 small apple	40
½ oz (15g) raisins	1 tablespoon raisins	35
½ oz (15g) walnuts	⅛ cup walnuts	75
2 fl oz (50ml) dairy or soya yogurt	¼ cup dairy or soy yogurt	30
1 teaspoon lemon juice	1 teaspoon lemon juice	
2 unbuttered brown rye crispbreads	2 unbuttered brown rye crispbreads	50
		259

Grate turnip, carrot, cabbage and apple. Combine with yogurt and lemon juice. Grind nuts and sprinkle on top. Serve with crispbread.

Dinner

RICEY MINCE

Imperial (Metric)	American	Calories
1 oz (25g) unflavoured mince-style TVP	1 ounce unflavored mince-style TVP	95
½ teaspoon yeast extract	½ teaspoon yeast extract	5
1 small onion	1 small onion	12
½ small green pepper	½ small green pepper	12
2 teaspoons vegetable oil	2 teaspoons vegetable oil	80
2 oz (50g) short-grain brown rice	⅓ cup brown rice	200
4 oz (100g) tinned tomatoes	4 ounces canned tomatoes	12
½ teaspoon marjoram	½ teaspoon marjoram	
2 oz (50g) mushrooms	1 cup mushrooms	5
1 bay leaf	1 bay leaf	
salt and pepper, to taste	salt and pepper, to taste	
		421
	Total	975

Soak the rice overnight. Chop and fry the onion and green pepper in the oil until tender. Add the mushrooms and *sauté* 3-4 minutes longer. Meanwhile, pour over the TVP just enough water to cover, mixing in yeast extract at the same time. Add rice and TVP to onion mixture and stir briefly. Add tomatoes, herbs and seasonings and enough water to cover the mixture. Bring to the boil, cover and simmer gently until rice is tender and liquid is absorbed.

MENU 6

Breakfast

HIGH PROTEIN CEREAL

Imperial (Metric)	American	Calories
1 oz (25g) wheat germ	¼ cup wheat germ	100
½ oz (15g) sunflower seeds	⅛ cup sunflower seeds	85
1 apple	1 small apple	50
½ oz (15g) sesame seeds	⅛ cup sesame seeds	80
¼ pint (150ml) skimmed milk or 4 fl oz (100ml) soya milk	⅔ cup skim milk or ½ cup soymilk	50
3 teaspoons clear honey	3 teaspoons honey	60
		425

Grind seeds in a blender, combine with wheat germ in a bowl. Add milk. Top with chopped apple and honey.

Lunch

BEANY COLESLAW

Imperial (Metric)	American	Calories
3 oz (75g) white cabbage	3 ounces white cabbage	25
1 tablespoon finely minced onion	1 tablespoon finely minced onion	10
1 small carrot	1 small carrot	
½ oz (15g) raisins	1 tablespoon raisins	35
1 small (or ½ large) eating apple	1 small (or ½ large) sweet apple	40
5 oz (125g) tinned baked beans	5 ounces canned vegetarian baked beans	125
		235

Grate cabbage and carrot coarsely, chop apple finely. Combine all ingredients and serve.

Dinner

MACARONI SAUTÉ

Imperial (Metric)	American	Calories
2 oz (50g) wholemeal macaroni	½ cup wholewheat macaroni	200
1 small onion	1 small onion	12
1 small clove garlic	1 small clove garlic	2
2 teaspoons vegetable oil	2 teaspoons vegetable oil	80
½ small green pepper	½ small green pepper	12
4 fl oz (100ml) tomato juice	½ cup tomato juice	20
salt and pepper, to taste	salt and pepper, to taste	
		326
	Total	986

Chop onion, green pepper and garlic. *Sauté* in oil until tender. Add macaroni and stir together for 5 minutes over low heat. Heat tomato juice to boil. Stir into macaroni mixture with seasoning to taste. Pour into baking dish. Cover. Bake at 350°F (180°C/Gas Mark 4) for 30-40 minutes.

MENU 7

Breakfast

Imperial (Metric)	American	Calories
¼ pint (150ml) orange juice	⅔ cup unsweetened orange juice	50

SCRAMBLED EGG OR TOFU, SAUSALATA AND TOMATO

Imperial (Metric)	American	Calories
scrambled egg made with 1 large egg and a few drops skimmed milk or scrambled tofu made by mashing 3 oz (75g) tofu with a teaspoon soya sauce and pinch turmeric	scrambled egg made with 1 large egg and a few drops skim milk or scrambled tofu made by mashing 3 ounces tofu with a teaspoon soy sauce and pinch turmeric	95
2 teaspoons vegetable margarine	2 teaspoons vegetable margarine	80
1 small tomato	2½ ounces tomato	10
1 Sausalata	1 vegetarian sausage	55
		290

Grill (broil) tomato and Sausalata . Serve with scrambled egg or tofu.

Lunch

CHICK PEA (GARBANZO BEAN) SALAD

Imperial (Metric)	American	Calories
2 oz (50g) chick peas	⅓ cup garbanzo beans	180
1 spring onion }	1 scallion }	10
1 stick celery	1 stalk celery	
½ oz (15g) chopped parsley	½ ounce chopped parsley	
1 teaspoon lemon juice	1 teaspoon lemon juice	
2 teaspoons vegetable oil	2 teaspoons vegetable oil	80
garlic salt, to taste	garlic salt, to taste	
2 slices unbuttered brown rye crispbread	2 slices unbuttered brown rye crispbread	50
		320

Soak chick peas (garbanzo beans) overnight, cook the next morning until soft. Cool. Drain off excess juice. Mince spring onion (scallion), dice celery, and chop parsley. Combine all ingredients and eat with crispbread.

Dinner

NUTTY STUFFED AUBERGINE (EGGPLANT)

Imperial (Metric)	American	Calories
8 oz (225g) aubergine	½ pound eggplant	30
1 teaspoon yeast extract	1 teaspoon yeast extract	10
1 small onion	1 small onion	12
2 oz (50g) cashew nuts	½ cup cashews	360
2 oz (50g) mushrooms	1 cup mushrooms	5
4 oz (100g) green beans	¼ pound green beans	15
		432
	Total	1042

Cook the washed aubergine (eggplant) in boiling water for 20-30 minutes. Finely chop the onion and mushrooms. Put in saucepan with yeast extract and just enough water to cover. Simmer until tender. Drain the liquid. Grind the cashews finely and mix with the onions and mushrooms. When aubergine (eggplant) is cool enough to handle, remove centre, chop and add to cashew mixture. Stuff aubergine (eggplant) shells with this and bake for 20 minutes at 400°F (200°C/Gas Mark 6). Serve accompanied by cooked green beans.

MENU 8

Breakfast

SWEET BANANA TOASTIES

Imperial (Metric)	American	Calories
2 slices wholemeal bread	2 slices wholewheat bread	130
1 heaped teaspoon raw sugar or sugar-free strawberry jam	1 heaped teaspoon raw sugar or sugar-free strawberry jam	25
1 teaspoon butter or vegetable margarine	1 teaspoon butter or vegetable margarine	40
1 small ripe banana	1 small ripe banana	45
		240

Toast the bread on one side only. Peel, slice and mash the banana. Butter the untoasted side of the bread; spread the other with jam and mashed banana. Put together, cut with a sharp knife and serve at once.

Lunch

CREAMY BEAN SOUP

Imperial (Metric)	American	Calories
4 oz (100g) cooked butter beans	4 ounces cooked lima beans	100
8 fl oz (225ml) liquid (juice from butter beans and tomatoes plus water)	1 cup liquid (juice from lima beans and tomatoes plus water)	5
4 oz (100g) tinned tomatoes	4 ounces canned tomatoes	12
garlic salt to taste	garlic salt to taste	
3 slices unbuttered brown rye crispbread	3 slices unbuttered brown rye cripsbread	75
		192

Pour all ingredients (except crispbread) into liquidizer. Liquidize thoroughly. Pour into saucepan and heat gently. Season to taste. Serve with the crispbread.

Dinner

MACARONI AND VEGETABLES

Imperial (Metric)	American	Calories
1 small onion	1 small onion	12
1 oz (25g) broken cashews	¼ cup broken cashews	180
1 small tomato	2½ ounces tomato	10
2 oz (50g) wholemeal macaroni	½ cup wholewheat macaroni	200
1 teaspoon lemon juice	1 teaspoon lemon juice	
2 teaspoons vegetable oil	2 teaspoons vegetable oil	80
1 oz (25g) raisins	1 ounce raisins	35
4 oz (100g) broccoli (fresh or frozen)	¼ pound broccoli (fresh or frozen)	15
salt to taste	salt to taste	
		532
	Total	964

Chop onion, *sauté* with cashews and raisins, in oil for 5 minutes. Slice tomato and add to pan. *Sauté* for 5-10 minutes longer. Add broccoli, lemon juice and salt. Cover and cook for approximately 10 minutes, until broccoli is tender. Add macaroni which has been cooked in boiling salted water until tender and then drained. Mix thoroughly.

MENU 9

Breakfast

Imperial (Metric)	American	Calories
¼ pint (150ml) orange juice	⅔ cup unsweetened orange juice	50
2 oz (50g) Grapenuts served with:	½ cup Grapenuts served with:	200
¼ pint (150ml) skimmed milk or 4 fl oz (100ml) soya milk	⅔ cup skim milk or ½ cup soymilk	50
1 teaspoon brown sugar	1 teaspoon brown sugar	17
		317

Lunch

BANANANUT SALAD

Imperial (Metric)	American	Calories
1 banana	1 banana	65
2 oz (50g) dairy or soya yogurt	¼ cup dairy or soy yogurt	30
1 teaspoon lemon juice	1 teaspoon lemon juice	
½ oz (15g) peanut butter	½ ounce peanut butter	90
a few lettuce leaves	a few lettuce leaves	
		185

Beat together yogurt, lemon juice and peanut butter. Peel banana and place on lettuce leaves. Top with peanut butter mixture.

Dinner

RICE DELIGHT

Imperial (Metric)	American	Calories
2 oz (50g) brown rice	⅓ cup brown rice	200
1 small carrot	1 small carrot	5
1 stick celery	1 stalk celery	2
1 small onion	1 small onion	12
1 small clove garlic	1 small clove garlic	2
½ oz (15g) raisins	1 tablespoon raisins	35
good pinch ginger	good pinch ginger	
½ oz (15g) sesame seeds	⅛ cup sesame seeds	80
½ small eating apple	½ small or ¼ large apple	25
½ oz (15g) walnut pieces	⅛ cup walnut pieces	75
2 teaspoons vegetable oil	2 teaspoons vegetable oil	80
Tamari (soya sauce), to taste	Tamari (soy sauce), to taste	5
pinch cinnamon	pinch cinnamon	
		521
	Total	1023

Soak rice and put on to cook gently. Chop all the vegetables finely and *sauté* in oil for 10-15 minutes. Add sesame seeds, walnuts and apple (which has been grated) and cook for another 5-10 minutes. When rice is nearly done add raisins to it. When rice is finished add Tamari to taste then add the vegetable mixture and the spices. Mix well and continue to cook for 5-10 minutes.

MENU 10

Breakfast

Imperial (Metric)	American	Calories
1 small pear	1 small pear	50

TAHINI OATCAKES

Imperial (Metric)	American	Calories
3 oatcakes	3 oatcakes	180
½ oz (15g) tahini	½ ounce tahini	85
½ oz (50g) honey	½ ounce honey	40
		355

Mix the tahini and honey together and spread over the oatcakes.

Lunch

CHILLI BEAN SOUP

Imperial (Metric)	American	Calories
4 oz (100g) cooked red kidney beans	4 ounces cooked red kidney beans	130
¼ pint (150ml) water	⅔ cup water	
1 tablespoon tomato purée	1 tablespoon tomato paste	10
½–1 teaspoon Mexican chilli seasoning	½–1 teaspoon Mexican chili seasoning	
1 small slice wholemeal bread, thinly buttered	1 small slice wholewheat bread, thinly buttered	100
		240

Put the beans, water, tomato *purée* (paste) and Mexican chilli (chili) seasoning into a small saucepan. Bring to the boil, then leave to simmer, uncovered, for a few minutes. Pour about two-thirds of the mixture from the pan into a liquidizer; leave to cool briefly, then blend thoroughly. Return to the remaining third in the saucepan, stir well, and re-heat gently. Serve with bread.

Dinner

MACARONI PEPERONATA

Imperial (Metric)	American	Calories
1 small onion	1 small onion	12
1 teaspoon vegetable margarine	1 teaspoon vegetable margarine	40
1 teaspoon olive oil	1 teaspoon olive oil	40
1 small red pepper	1 small red pepper	24
½ small green pepper	½ small green pepper	12
1 small clove garlic	1 small clove garlic	5
4 oz (100g) ripe tomatoes	¼ pound ripe tomatoes	16
2½ oz (65g) wholemeal macaroni	⅓ cup wholewheat macaroni	250
2 teaspoons Parmesan cheese or nutritional yeast	2 teaspoons Parmesan cheese or nutritional yeast	25
		424
	Total	1019

Chop the onion finely. Heat the margarine and oil in a small saucepan and add the onion. *Sauté* until beginning to brown. Slice the peppers very thinly. Add them to the saucepan, cover pan and simmer over a very low heat for about 10 minutes. Chop the garlic finely. Skin and chop the tomatoes. Add them to the pan and cook, covered, over low heat for about 20 minutes, stirring occasionally. Meanwhile, cook the macaroni in a largish pan, then drain it, return it to the pan, and mix in the peperonata. Sprinkle the cheese or yeast over the top.

MENU 11

Breakfast

Imperial (Metric)	American	Calories
2 oz (50g) Muesli	½ cup Muesli	220
¼ pint (150ml) skimmed milk or 4 fl oz (100ml) soya milk	⅔ cup skim milk or ½ cup soymilk	50
1 grated apple	1 small grated apple	50
		320

Lunch

TOFU SLICES ON TOAST WITH CREAMY GRAVY

Imperial (Metric)	American	Calories
3 oz (75g) firm tofu	3 ounces firm tofu	90
1 tablespoon Tamari (soya sauce)	1 tablespoon Tamari (soy sauce)	5
1 teaspoon sesame oil (available at Chinese shops)	1 teaspoon sesame oil (available at Chinese shops)	40
pinch ginger	pinch ginger	
½ oz (15g) rolled oats	⅛ cup rolled oats	50
½ teaspoon vegetable oil	½ teaspoon vegetable oil	20
1 teaspoon miso	1 teaspoon miso	25
¼ pint (150ml) warm water	⅔ cup warm water	
freshly ground black pepper	freshly ground black pepper	
2 slices wholemeal toast	2 slices wholewheat toast	130
		360

Slice the tofu thinly. Combine in a shallow bowl the soya (soy) sauce, sesame oil, ginger and 1 tablespoon water. Marinate the tofu slices in this for a few minutes (or longer), turning occasionally. Grill (broil) the slices, basting from time to time and turning once or twice, until nicely browned. Meanwhile, grind the rolled oats in a blender. Add the vegetable oil, miso, and warm water and blend well. Pour into a small saucepan and cook over gentle heat, stirring constantly until thickened. Season with pepper. Place the tofu slices on the toast and pour the gravy over them.

Dinner

YOGURTY MUSHROOM AND COURGETTE (ZUCCHINI) CURRY

Imperial (Metric)	American	Calories
2 oz (110g) brown rice	⅓ cup brown rice	200
1 small onion	1 small onion	12
1 clove garlic	1 clove garlic	2
2 teaspoons vegetable oil	2 teaspoons vegetable oil	80
1 teaspoon curry powder	1 teaspoon curry powder	
4 oz (100g) mushrooms	2 cups mushrooms	8
1 small courgette	1 small zucchini	12
3 oz (75g) dairy or soya yogurt	⅓ cup dairy or soy yogurt	45
		359
	Total	1039

Cook the rice. Chop the onion and crush the garlic. *Sauté* onion and garlic in the oil until softened. Stir in the curry powder. Slice the mushrooms and courgette (zucchini). Add them to the saucepan along with a tablespoon of water. Stir well, cover and cook over low heat for 5-7 minutes. Stir in the yogurt and cook uncovered for a further 3-5 minutes. Serve over the cooked brown rice.

MENU 12

Breakfast

Imperial (Metric)	American	Calories
4 fl oz (100ml) orange juice	½ cup orange juice	50

OATMEAL PORRIDGE

Imperial (Metric)	American	Calories
2 oz (50g) medium oatmeal	½ cup medium oatmeal	200
water and sea salt, to taste	water and sea salt, to taste	
⅛ pint (70ml) skimmed or soya milk	⅓ cup skim or soy milk	25
2 teaspoons raw sugar	2 teaspoons raw sugar	34
		309

Pour oatmeal into about 3 times its volume in water (the exact amount will depend on whether one prefers a thin or thick porridge). Bring the water and oatmeal to the boil and add salt to taste. Lower heat and simmer uncovered for 5-10 minutes. Serve topped with the milk and sugar.

Lunch

PASTA SALAD*

Imperial (Metric)	American	Calories
2 oz (50g) wholemeal macaroni or other pasta shapes	½ cup wholewheat macaroni or other pasta shapes	200
6 oz (175g) Morinaga silken tofu	¾ cup silken tofu	76
1-2 teaspoons lemon juice	1-2 teaspoons lemon juice	
½ teaspoon Tamari (soya sauce)	½ teaspoon Tamari (soy sauce)	
1 stick celery	1 stalk celery	5
1 spring onion	1 scallion	2
¼ red pepper	¼ red pepper	20
3 black olives	3 black olives	15
		318

*A version of this recipe first appeared in *Green Cuisine* magazine (September/October, 1986).

Cook the pasta in lightly-salted boiling water until just tender.
Drain and rinse. Put the tofu, lemon juice and soya (soy) sauce in a
liquidizer and blend thoroughly. Chop the celery, spring onion
(scallion), red pepper and olives finely. Combine the pasta with the
tofu dressing and the chopped vegetables. Chill before serving.

Dinner

TOASTY PIZZA

Imperial (Metric)	American	Calories
1 tablespoon olive oil	1 tablespoon olive oil	120
1 onion	1 onion	24
4 oz (100g) tomatoes	¼ pound tomatoes	16
small clove garlic	small clove garlic	2
1 teaspoon tomato purée	1 teaspoon tomato paste	4
1 tablespoon minced parsley	1 tablespoon minced parsley	
1 teaspoon dried oregano	1 teaspoon dried oregano	
1 teaspoon miso	1 teaspoon miso	25
1 teaspoon tahini	1 teaspoon tahini	30
3 small slices wholemeal bread	3 small slices wholewheat bread	120
1 tablespoon Parmesan cheese or nutritional yeast	1 tablespoon Parmesan cheese or nutritional yeast	30
		371
	Total	998

Chop the onion. *Sauté* in the oil for a few minutes over a low heat
until softening. Skin and chop the tomatoes. Chop the garlic finely.
Add the tomatoes, garlic, tomato *purée* (paste), parsley and oregano;
cover the pan and cook over lowest possible heat for 10-15 minutes,
stirring occasionally. Stir in the miso and tahini. Toast the bread
lightly, then top with the tomato mixture. Sprinkle cheese or yeast
over the top, then place under a hot grill (broiler) for 2-3 minutes
before serving.

MENU 13

Breakfast

Imperial (Metric)	American	Calories
4 fl oz (100ml) orange juice	½ cup orange juice	50

SEMOLINA (FARINA) PORRIDGE WITH STRAWBERRY JAM

Imperial (Metric)	American	Calories
8 fl oz (225ml) skimmed milk or 6 fl oz (175ml) soya milk diluted with 2 fl oz (50ml) water	1 cup skim milk or ¾ cup soymilk diluted with ¼ cup water	75
1 oz (25g) wholemeal semolina	¼ cup wholewheat farina	100
2 teaspoons raw sugar or sugar-free strawberry jam	2 teaspoons raw sugar or sugar-free strawberry jam	34
		259

Heat the milk (or milk and water) slowly in a saucepan, and stir in the semolina (farina). Bring to the boil, stirring constantly, then lower heat and leave to simmer uncovered for 3-4 minutes. Serve topped with the jam.

Lunch

MISO SOUP WITH TOFU

Imperial (Metric)	American	Calories
1 small onion	1 small onion	12
2 teaspoons vegetable oil	2 teaspoons vegetable oil	80
¼ pint (150ml) water	⅔ cup water	
1 teaspoon miso	1 teaspoon miso	25
4 oz (100g) Morinaga silken tofu	½ cup silken tofu	52
2 slices wholemeal bread, thinly spread with vegetable margarine	2 slices wholewheat bread, thinly spread with vegetable margarine	200
		369

Chop the onion and *sauté* in the vegetable oil in a small saucepan until beginning to brown. Add the water, bring to the boil, then simmer for a few minutes. Remove a little of the water from the saucepan and cream it with the miso in a cup. Dice the tofu. Add the creamed miso and the tofu to the saucepan. Cook briefly at the lowest possible temperature until heated through. Serve with the bread (toasted if preferred).

Dinner

SPANISH-STYLE BULGUR WHEAT*

Imperial (Metric)	American	Calories
1 teaspoon vegetable oil	1 teaspoon vegetable oil	40
2 oz (50g) bulgur wheat	½ cup bulgur wheat	204
1 small leek	1 small leek	18
½ small green pepper	½ small green pepper	12
4 oz (100g) tinned tomatoes	4 ounces canned tomatoes	12
¼ pint (150ml) water	⅔ cup water	
4 oz (100g) cooked haricot beans	4 ounces cooked navy beans	108
pinch garlic salt	pinch garlic salt	
½ teaspoon paprika	½ teaspoon paprika	
pinch cayenne pepper (optional)	pinch cayenne (optional)	
		394
	Total	1022

Heat the oil gently and add the bulgur wheat. Stir until beginning to turn golden. Chop the leek and green pepper finely. Chop the tomatoes coarsely. Add the tomatoes with a little of their liquid along with all the rest of the ingredients to the bulgur wheat. Bring to the boil, lower heat and simmer for 15 minutes. After the first 5 minutes check to make sure that the liquid has not yet all been absorbed; if it has then add a little more water.

*A version of this recipe originally appeared in *Green Cuisine* magazine (September/October, 1986).

WINTER MENUS

MENU 1

Breakfast

Imperial (Metric)	American	Calories
2 oz (50g) Granola-type cereal	½ cup Granola-type cereal	260
served with:	served with:	
1 grated apple	1 small grated apple	50
¼ pint (150ml) skimmed milk or 4 fl oz (100ml) soya milk	⅔ cup skim milk or ½ cup soymilk	50
		360

Lunch

SPINACH AND YOGURT SALAD

Imperial (Metric)	American	Calories
4 fl oz (100ml) dairy or soya yogurt	½ cup dairy or soy yogurt	60
4 oz (100g) raw spinach	4 ounces raw spinach	15
¼ small red pepper	¼ small red pepper	10
¼ bunch watercress	¼ bunch watercress	5
1 teaspoon chopped parsley	1 teaspoon chopped parsley	
¼ oz (7g) Smokey Snaps	¼ ounce imitation bacon bits	25
celery salt, garlic salt and pepper, to taste	celery salt, garlic salt and pepper, to taste	
2 slices brown rye crispbread, thinly spread with vegetable margarine	2 slices brown rye crispbread, thinly spread with vegetable margarine	100
		215

Mix yogurt with seasonings and parsley. Tear spinach into pieces, cut red pepper into strips. Combine spinach, red pepper and watercress. Toss in yogurt mixture. Top with Smokey Snaps (imitation bacon bits).

Dinner

SPAGHETTI NAPOLETANA

Imperial (Metric)	American	Calories
2½ oz (65g) wholemeal spaghetti	2½ ounces wholewheat spaghetti	250
½ green pepper	½ green pepper	20
1 small onion	1 small onion	12
2 oz (50g) mushrooms	1 cup mushrooms	5
1 heaped teaspoon tomato purée	1 heaped teaspoon tomato paste	5
1 tablespoon Parmesan cheese or nutritional yeast	1 tablespoon Parmesan cheese or nutritional yeast	30
2 teaspoons vegetable oil	2 teaspoons vegetable oil	80
1 small carrot 1 small clove garlic	1 small carrot 1 small clove garlic	10
4 oz (100g) tinned tomatoes	4 ounces canned tomatoes	12
1 teaspoon oregano	1 teaspoon oregano	
		424
	Total	999

Cook spaghetti in boiling salted water until tender. Chop onion and green pepper finely, slice mushrooms, crush garlic and finely grate carrot. Fry all together in oil for 5-10 minutes. Add tomatoes, *purée* (paste) and oregano. Cook until it becomes a thick sauce. Drain spaghetti, pour sauce over and sprinkle with cheese or yeast.

MENU 2

Breakfast

Imperial (Metric)	American	Calories
¼ pint (150ml) orange juice	⅔ cup orange juice	50

OATMEAL PORRIDGE

Imperial (Metric)	American	Calories
2 oz (50g) medium oatmeal	½ cup medium oatmeal	200
salt and water, to taste (depending on how thick the porridge is preferred)	salt and water, to taste (depending on how thick the porridge is preferred)	
⅛ pint (65ml) skimmed milk or 2 fl oz (50ml) soya milk	⅓ cup skim milk or ¼ cup soymilk	25
1 teaspoon brown sugar	1 teaspoon brown sugar	17
		292

Pour oatmeal into about 3 times its volume in water (the exact amount will depend on whether one prefers a thin or thick porridge). Bring the water and oatmeal to the boil and add salt to taste, lower heat and simmer uncovered for 5-10 minutes. Serve topped with milk and sugar.

Lunch

SPINACH SOUP

Imperial (Metric)	American	Calories
4 oz (100g) fresh spinach	4 ounces fresh spinach	15
½ vegetable stock cube	½ vegetable bouillon cube	15
1 slice wholemeal bread with thin spreading of vegetable margarine	1 slice wholewheat bread with thin spreading of vegetable margarine	100
½ pint (285ml) hot water	1⅓ cups hot water	
		130

Wash spinach thoroughly and cook in the water that clings to the leaves. Turn the cooked spinach into the liquidizer and *purée*. Sieve if desired. Combine with water and stock cube and bring gently to the boil. Serve with slice of bread.

Dinner

NUT JAMBALAYA

Imperial (Metric)	American	Calories
2 oz (50g) brown rice	⅓ cup brown rice	200
2 teaspoons vegetable oil	2 teaspoons vegetable oil	80
1 small tomato	2½ ounces tomato	10
½ oz (15g) chopped almonds	⅛ cup chopped almonds	80
3 oz (75g) cooked red kidney beans	3 ounces cooked red kidney beans	99
½ green pepper	½ green pepper	16
½ oz (15g) desiccated coconut	½ ounce grated coconut	90
salt to taste	salt to taste	
		575
	Total	997

Cook the rice. Chop the pepper and tomato. *Sauté* 3-5 minutes in the oil. Add nuts and coconut and *sauté* a further three minutes. Add cooked beans and a little of the liquid and simmer gently. Season to taste and serve on top of rice.

MENU 3

Breakfast

Imperial (Metric)	American	Calories
2 oz (50g) muesli	½ cup muesli	220
served with:	served with:	
1 small thinly sliced banana	1 small thinly sliced banana	55
¼ pint (150ml) skimmed milk or 4 fl oz (100ml) soya milk	⅔ cup skim milk or ½ cup soymilk	50
		325

Lunch

PROVENÇAL SOUP

Imperial (Metric)	American	Calories
2 teaspoons vegetable oil	2 teaspoons vegetable oil	80
½ small clove garlic	½ small clove garlic	
1 oz (25g) celery	1 ounce celery	2
1 tablespoon chopped onion	1 tablespoon chopped onion	5
3 oz (75g) tomatoes	3 ounces tomatoes	12
mixed herbs, to taste	mixed herbs, to taste	
½ oz (15g) short-grain brown rice	½ ounce brown rice	50
salt and pepper, to taste	salt and pepper, to taste	
½ pint (¼ litre) water	1⅓ cups water	
		149

Mince celery. Peel and chop tomatoes. Chop garlic. *Sauté* onion, celery, garlic and tomatoes in oil for 5 minutes. Add herbs, water, rice and seasoning. Simmer for 45 minutes to an hour.

Dinner

SPAGHETTI AND BUTTER (LIMA) BEAN CASSEROLE

Imperial (Metric)	American	Calories
2½ oz (65g) wholemeal spaghetti	2½ ounces wholewheat spaghetti	250
1 small onion	1 small onion	12
1 small clove garlic	1 small clove garlic	2
½ small green or red pepper	½ red or green pepper	16
4 oz (100g) tinned tomatoes	4 ounces canned tomatoes	12
½ teaspoon brown sugar	½ teaspoon brown sugar	15
¼ teaspoon thyme	¼ teaspoon thyme	
1 oz (25g) fresh wholemeal breadcrumbs	½ cup fresh wholewheat breadcrumbs	65
3 oz (75g) cooked butter beans	3 ounces cooked lima beans	78
2 teaspoons vegetable oil	2 teaspoons vegetable oil	80
1 tablespoon tomato purée	1 tablespoon tomato paste	10
¼ teaspoon oregano	¼ teaspoon oregano	
1 tablespoon minced parsley	1 tablespoon minced parsley	
		540
	Total	1014

Cook spaghetti in boiling salted water until tender. Chop onion, garlic and pepper finely and *sauté* in oil until tender. Sieve the tomatoes, add to vegetables along with *purée* (paste), sugar and herbs. Simmer at low heat 15-20 minutes. Layer cooked spaghetti, beans and tomato sauce in a casserole dish. Top with breadcrumbs. Bake at 350°F (180°C/Gas Mark 4) for 45 minutes to an hour.

MENU 4

Breakfast

Imperial (Metric)	American	Calories
¼ pint (150ml) grapefruit juice	⅔ cup grapefruit juice	50
2 oz (50g) Grapenuts served with:	½ cup Grapenuts served with:	200
¼ pint (150ml) skimmed milk or 4 fl oz (100ml) soya milk	⅔ cup skim milk or ½ cup soymilk	50
2 teaspoons brown sugar	2 teaspoons brown sugar	34
		334

Lunch

CABBAGE APPLE SALAD

Imperial (Metric)	American	Calories
2 oz (50g) cabbage	2 ounces cabbage	15
1 small apple	1 small apple	40
1 stick celery	1 stalk celery	
½ small raw beetroot }	½ small raw beet }	15
1 small carrot	1 small carrot	
¼ oz (7g) raisins	¼ ounce raisins	20
1 small banana	1 small banana	45
2 teaspoons vegetable oil	2 teaspoons vegetable oil	80
1 teaspoon lemon juice	1 teaspoon lemon juice	
1 slice wholemeal bread, thinly spread with vegetable margarine	1 slice wholewheat bread, thinly spread with vegetable margarine	100
		315

Mince celery; grate carrot, apple and beetroot (beet); shred cabbage. Mix together with raisins. For dressing, mash banana, add oil and lemon juice and beat well with fork. Combine with salad. Eat with slice of bread.

Dinner

BUTTER (LIMA) BEAN AND VEGETABLE CASSEROLE

Imperial (Metric)	American	Calories
3 oz (75g) cooked butter beans	3 ounces cooked lima beans	78
1 small carrot ⎱ 2 sticks celery ⎰	1 small carrot ⎱ 2 stalks celery ⎰	10
2 teaspoons vegetable margarine	2 teaspoons vegetable margarine	80
½ teaspoon mixed herbs	½ teaspoon mixed herbs	
1 small onion	1 small onion	12
2 oz (50g) cauliflower	2 ounces cauliflower	15
4 oz (100g) potatoes	4 ounces potatoes	100
½ teaspoon yeast extract	½ teaspoon yeast extract	5
4 oz (100g) tinned tomatoes	4 ounces canned tomatoes	12
½ oz (15g) fresh wholemeal breadcrumbs	¼ cup fresh wholewheat breadcrumbs	35
		347
	Total	996

Slice onion thinly and *sauté* in the margarine. Chop rest of vegetables and add these to the pan, stirring over a moderate heat. Add beans, yeast extract, herbs and tomatoes. Bring to the boil and put into casserole dish. Cover and bake in a moderate oven 350°F (180°C/Gas Mark 4) for an hour and a half. Remove lid from casserole, sprinkle breadcrumbs over the top and cook for a further 20 minutes until topping is crisp.

MENU 5

Breakfast

Imperial (Metric)	American	Calories
4 fl oz (150ml) unsweetened orange juice	½ cup orange juice	40

TAHINI TOAST

Imperial (Metric)	American	Calories
1 oz (25g) tahini	1 ounce tahini	170
½ oz (15g) honey	½ ounce honey	40
2 slices wholemeal bread	2 slices wholewheat bread	130
		380

Mix tahini with honey. Toast bread and spread with tahini/honey mixture.

Lunch

TOMATO AND LEEK SOUP

Imperial (Metric)	American	Calories
8 oz (225g) tinned tomatoes	8 ounces canned tomatoes	24
2 teaspoons vegetable oil	2 teaspoons vegetable oil	80
½ pint (275ml) vegetable stock or water	1⅓ cups vegetable stock or water	
1 small leek	1 small leek	20
½ teaspoon basil or marjoram	½ teaspoon sweet basil or marjoram	
salt to taste	salt to taste	
1 small slice wholemeal bread (thinly buttered)	1 small slice wholewheat bread (thinly buttered)	100
		224

Chop the leek finely and cook in the oil for a few minutes. Chop the tomatoes roughly and add to pan with juice from tomatoes and stock or water as well as herbs. Bring to the boil and simmer until cooked. Serve with the slice of bread.

Dinner

VEGETABLE CURRY

Imperial (Metric)	American	Calories
2½ oz (65g) brown rice	2½ ounces brown rice	250
2 oz (65g) mushrooms	1 cup mushrooms	5
4 oz (100g) tomatoes	4 ounces tomatoes	15
1 teaspoon curry powder (or to taste)	1 teaspoon curry powder (or to taste)	
4 oz (100g) frozen mixed vegetables	4 ounces frozen mixed vegetables	30
2 teaspoons vegetable margarine	2 teaspoons vegetable margarine	80
1 small onion	1 small onion	12
salt to taste	salt to taste	
		392
	Total	996

Soak rice and cook in boiling salted water. Chop onion and mushrooms and *sauté* in margarine until tender. Add curry powder and cook for two minutes longer, stirring constantly. Add skinned chopped tomatoes and cook for an additional 3-5 minutes. Add frozen vegetables and just enough water to barely cover them. Stir well, simmer till tender. Serve over rice.

MENU 6

Breakfast

APPLE AND RAISIN BREAKFAST

Imperial (Metric)	American	Calories
1 apple	1 small apple	50
2 oz (50g) raisins	⅓ cup raisins	140
juice of ½ lemon	juice of ½ lemon	5
2 tablespoons single cream (or undiluted tinned or double-strength powdered soya milk)	2 tablespoons light cream (or rich soymilk or double-strength powdered soymilk)	60
½ oz (15g) wholewheat flakes	½ ounce wholewheat flakes	50
½ oz (15g) brown sugar	½ ounce brown sugar	50
		355

Grate apple. Cook gently for 5 minutes in the lemon juice. Mix in raisins and cream. Place in cereal bowl. Top with flakes and sugar.

Lunch

WALNUT SALAD

Imperial (Metric)	American	Calories
1 oz (25g) walnut pieces	¼ cup walnut pieces	150
2 teaspoons lemon juice or cider vinegar	2 teaspoons lemon juice or cider vinegar	
1 tablespoon vegetable oil	1 tablespoon vegetable oil	120
garlic or onion salt, to taste	garlic or onion salt, to taste	
a few leaves Cos lettuce	a few leaves Romaine lettuce	
1 small carrot	1 small carrot	
1 small courgette	1 small zucchini	25
1 small tomato	1 cherry tomato	
1 oz (25g) raw mushrooms	½ cup raw mushrooms	
		295

Shred lettuce finely; grate carrot; chop courgette (zucchini), tomato and mushrooms. Make dressing from oil, lemon juice and seasoning. Mix with salad. Top with walnuts (toasted if preferred).

Dinner

BUTTER (LIMA) BEAN ZESTY BAKE

Imperial (Metric)	American	Calories
4 oz (100g) cooked butter beans	4 ounces cooked lima beans	104
½ small green pepper	½ small green pepper	12
1 small onion	1 small onion	12
1 tablespoon vegetable margarine	1 tablespoon vegetable margarine	120
1 tablespoon wholemeal flour	1 tablespoon wholewheat flour	50
½ teaspoon brown sugar	½ teaspoon brown sugar	9
2 teaspoons cider vinegar	2 teaspoons cider vinegar	
¼ pint (150ml) tomato juice	⅓ cup tomato juice	30
¼ teaspoon dried mustard	¼ teaspoon mustard powder	
salt and pepper, to taste	salt and pepper, to taste	
		337
	Total	987

Chop the onion and green pepper finely and brown in the margarine. Add the flour, cook for a minute, then slowly add the tomato juice, stirring well to avoid lumps. Add the brown sugar, mustard, vinegar and seasonings, then mix in the beans. Place in a casserole dish and bake in a 375°F (190°C/Gas Mark 5) oven for 45 minutes.

MENU 7

Breakfast

Imperial (Metric)	American	Calories
¼ pint (150ml) orange juice	⅔ cup orange juice	50

SCRAMBLED EGG OR TOFU, SAUSALATA AND TOMATO

Imperial (Metric)	American	Calories
scrambled egg made with 1 large egg and a few drops skimmed milk; or scrambled tofu made by mashing 3 oz (75g) tofu with 1 teaspoon soya sauce and a pinch turmeric	scrambled egg made with 1 large egg and a few drops skim milk; or scrambled tofu made by mashing 3 ounces tofu with 1 teaspoon soy sauce and a pinch turmeric	95
2 teaspoons vegetable margarine	2 teaspoons vegetable margarine	80
2 oz (50g) mushrooms	1 cup mushrooms	5
1 Sausalata	1 vegetarian sausage	55
		285

Grill mushrooms and Sausalata (vegetarian sausage). Serve with scrambled egg or tofu.

Lunch

FRUIT AND NUT COLESLAW

Imperial (Metric)	American	Calories
2 oz (50g) white cabbage	2 ounces white cabbage	15
¼ small green pepper	¼ small green pepper	6
1 eating apple	1 small apple	50
½ oz (15g) raisins	1½ tablespoons raisins	35
2 teaspoons lemon juice	2 teaspoons lemon juice	
1 small carrot	1 small carrot	5
1 tablespoon finely chopped onion	1 tablespoon minced onion	5

Imperial (Metric)	American	Calories
1 oz (25g) roasted peanuts	¼ cup roasted peanuts	170
1 tablespoon vegetable oil	1 tablespoon vegetable oil	120
		406

Grate cabbage, carrot and apple. Mince green pepper. Combine with nuts and raisins and mix well with vinaigrette made from oil and lemon juice.

Dinner

VEGETABLE STEW

Imperial (Metric)	American	Calories
1 small onion	1 small onion	12
2 oz (50g) mushrooms	1 cup mushrooms	5
4 oz (100g) Jerusalem artichokes	4 ounces Jerusalem artichokes	30
2 oz (50g) black-eyed beans	2 ounces black-eyed peas	170
½ teaspoon yeast extract	½ teaspoon yeast extract	5
1 small leek	1 small leek	20
2 teaspoons vegetable oil	2 teaspoons vegetable oil	80
½ teaspoon mixed herbs	½ teaspoon mixed herbs	
1 teaspoon arrowroot powder	1 teaspoon arrowroot	25
		347
	Total	1038

Chop onion and leek and fry in oil until becoming tender. Chop and add mushrooms and artichokes. Add black-eyed beans (peas) which have been soaked overnight. Add yeast extract and herbs and just enough water to cover. Simmer until beans are tender (30–45 minutes). Put arrowroot in a cup, mix with a little water and add to the stew, stirring until thickened.

MENU 8

Breakfast

SWISS BREAKFAST

Imperial (Metric)	American	Calories
2 oz (50g) raisins	⅓ cup raisins	140
1 tablespoon honey	1 tablespoon honey	55
½ oz (15g) rolled oats	½ ounce rolled oats	50
1 apple	1 small apple	50
1 tablespoon single cream (or undiluted tinned or double-strength powdered soya milk)	1 tablespoon light cream (or rich soymilk or double-strength powdered soymilk)	30
		325

Cover raisins with boiling water and leave to soak overnight. Grate apple and stir into raisins with all other ingredients.

Lunch

CELERY AND BANANA SALAD

Imperial (Metric)	American	Calories
3 oz (75g) celery	3 ounces celery	10
1 small banana	1 small banana	45
¼ oz (7g) walnuts	¼ ounce walnuts	40
1 teaspoon honey	1 teaspoon honey	20
2 teaspoons single cream (or undiluted tinned or double-strength powdered soya milk)	2 teaspoons light cream (or rich soymilk or double-strength powdered soymilk)	20
1 teaspoon lemon juice	1 teaspoon lemon juice	
		135

Chop the celery finely and add the lemon juice. Mash the banana and mix it well with the celery. Beat in the cream or milk and honey. Top with walnuts.

Dinner

POTATO FRY

Imperial (Metric)	American	Calories
2 teaspoons vegetable margarine	2 teaspoons vegetable margarine	80
2 oz (50g) mushrooms	1 cup mushrooms	5
1½ oz (40g) hazelnuts	1½ ounces hazelnuts	270
mustard and cress or alfalfa sprouts	alfalfa sprouts or cress	5
1 medium onion	1 medium onion	24
6 oz (175g) potatoes	6 ounces potatoes	150
1 tablespoon chopped parsley	1 tablespoon chopped parsley	
salt and pepper, to taste	salt and pepper, to taste	
		534
	Total	994

Cook potatoes until just tender (it is not necessary to peel them).
Chop onions and mushrooms, fry in melted margarine until tender.
Dice potatoes and add to pan, continue to fry gently until golden
brown, stirring frequently. Add whole nuts (which may be toasted
under the grill first if desired), seasoning and parsley and mix gently.
Top with cress or sprouts.

MENU 9

Breakfast

ISLAND BREAKFAST CEREAL

Imperial (Metric)	American	Calories
¾ oz (20g) hazelnuts	¾ ounce hazelnuts	135
¾ oz (20g) almonds	¾ ounce almonds	120
1 oz (25g) rolled oats	¼ cup rolled oats	105
½ oz (25g) wheat germ	⅛ cup wheat germ	50
½ oz (15g) currants	½ ounce currants	70
½ oz (15g) dried apricots	½ ounce dried apricots	25
1 heaped teaspoon brown sugar	1 heaped teaspoon brown sugar	25
¼ pint (150ml) skimmed milk or 4 fl oz (100ml) soya milk	⅔ cup skim milk or ½ cup soymilk	50
		580

Spread the hazelnuts and almonds on a tray and bake in a moderate oven for 5-10 minutes. Remove skins from hazelnuts. Chop nuts and apricots. Combine all the dried ingredients and serve with the milk.

Lunch

GREEN PEPPER, CELERY AND MUSHROOM SALAD

Imperial (Metric)	American	Calories
2 oz (50g) celery	2 ounces celery	5
2 oz (50g) mushrooms	1 cup mushrooms	5
½ small green pepper	½ small green pepper	12
1 tablespoon onion, finely chopped	1 tablespoon minced onion	5
1 tablespoon vegetable oil	1 tablespoon vegetable oil	120
2 teaspoons cider vinegar	2 teaspoons cider vinegar	
pinch mustard powder	pinch mustard powder	

Imperial (Metric)	American	Calories
2 slices brown rye crispbread, thinly spread with vegetable margarine	2 slices brown rye crispbread, thinly spread with vegetable margarine	100
		247

Slice the celery, green pepper and mushrooms finely; place with onion in a bowl. Mix oil, vinegar and mustard, adding salt and pepper to taste. Pour the dressing over the salad and mix well. Leave it to stand for 2-3 hours and serve with crispbread.

Dinner

STUFFED GREEN PEPPER

Imperial (Metric)	American	Calories
1 oz (25g) brown rice	⅙ cup brown rice	100
½ teaspoon mixed herbs	½ teaspoon mixed herbs	
1 small carrot	1 small carrot	10
½ small onion	½ small onion	6
1 green pepper	1 green pepper	32
vegetable stock as required	vegetable stock as required	
2 teaspoons Parmesan cheese or nutritional yeast	2 teaspoons Parmesan cheese or nutritional yeast	25
		173
	Total	1000

Soak rice for a few hours and drain. Grate carrot finely and chop onion finely. Mix together rice, herbs, carrot and onion, add just enough boiling vegetable stock to cover and simmer until tender. Meanwhile, cook green pepper in boiling water for 5-10 minutes. Rinse in cold water, and, when cool enough to handle, remove top of pepper with stem and seeds. Fill with cooked rice mixture and place in baking dish. Cook in moderate oven 350°F (180°C/(Gas Mark 4) for 30 minutes. Serve topped with cheese or yeast.

MENU 10

Breakfast

GRAPENUT MUESLI

Imperial (Metric)	American	Calories
1½ oz (40g) rolled oats	1½ ounces rolled oats	150
½ oz (15g) Grapenuts	⅛ cup Grapenuts	50
1 teaspoon raw cane sugar	1 teaspoon raw cane sugar	20
½ oz (15g) peanuts	⅛ cup peanuts	80
½ oz (15g) raisins	1 tablespoon raisins	35
¼ pint (150ml) skimmed milk or 4 fl oz (100ml) soya milk or a mixture of milk and yogurt	⅔ cup skim milk or ½ cup soymilk or a mixture of milk and yogurt	50
		385

Combine all the dry ingredients, with milk (or milk and yogurt) poured over the mixture.

Lunch

YOGURT CHEESE WITH CHIVES

Imperial (Metric)	American	Calories
8 oz (225g) dairy or soya yogurt	1 cup dairy or soy yogurt	120
1-2 tablespoons minced chives or spring onion	1-2 tablespoons minced chives or scallion	
3 slices brown rye crispbread	3 slices brown rye crispbread	75
		195

Pour the yogurt into a large square of muslin or cheesecloth. Tie the ends onto the taps of a sink or basin and leave to drip for several hours or overnight. Place the cheesecloth onto some kitchen paper (paper towels) to soak up additional liquid, and leave in the fridge like that until ready to use. Mix the chives or spring onion (scallion) into the 'cheese', divide into 3 portions, and spread onto the crispbread.

Dinner

BUTTER (LIMA) BEANS AND MUSHROOMS AU GRATIN

Imperial (Metric)	American	Calories
4 oz (100g) cooked butter beans	4 ounces cooked lima beans	104
½ teaspoon lemon juice	½ teaspoon lemon juice	
4 oz (100g) mushrooms	2 cups mushrooms	10
1 tablespoon vegetable margarine	1 tablespoon vegetable margarine	120
1 tablespoon wholemeal flour	1 tablespoon wholewheat flour	50
¼ pint (150ml) skimmed milk or 4 fl oz (100ml) soya milk diluted with 1 fl oz (25ml) water	⅔ cup skim milk or ½ cup soymilk diluted with 1 fluid ounce water	50
salt and pepper	salt and pepper	
1 oz (25g) fresh wholemeal breadcrumbs	½ cup fresh wholewheat breadcrumbs	65
2 teaspoons Parmesan cheese or nutritional yeast	2 teaspoons Parmesan cheese or nutritional yeast	25
3 oz (75g) Brussels sprouts	3 ounces Brussels sprouts	21
		445
	Total	1025

Place the beans on the bottom of an oven dish. Sprinkle with the lemon juice. Chop the mushrooms. Heat the margarine in a saucepan. Add the mushrooms and *sauté* for a few minutes until tender. Stir in the flour, then stir in the milk very gradually, stirring constantly over a medium heat to avoid lumps. When it has thickened and is boiling add seasoning to taste. Pour the mushroom sauce over the beans. Sprinkle the breadcrumbs on top and then finally the cheese or yeast. Bake at 375°F (190°C/Gas Mark 5) for about 20 minutes. Meanwhile, cook the Brussels sprouts and serve as a vegetable accompaniment.

MENU 11

Breakfast

Imperial (Metric)	American	Calories
1 small fresh orange	1 small fresh orange	40

SAVOURY MIX

Imperial (Metric)	American	Calories
2 oz (50g) smoked tofu	2 ounces smoked tofu	60
2 oz (50g) mushrooms	1 cup mushrooms	5
1 small tomato	2½ ounces tomato	10
2 teaspoons vegetable oil	2 teaspoons vegetable oil	80
1 small slice wholemeal toast	1 small slice wholewheat toast	65
		260

Slice the tofu as thinly as possible. Slice the mushrooms and tomato. Heat the oil in a frying pan and fry the tofu, mushrooms and tomato, turning to cook evenly. Serve piled onto the toast.

Lunch

POTATO AND VEGETABLE SALAD

Imperial (Metric)	American	Calories
4 oz (100g) potatoes	4 ounces potatoes	100
3 oz (75g) Morinaga silken tofu	3 ounces silken tofu	38
1 teaspoon lemon juice	1 teaspoon lemon juice	
1½ teaspoons vegetable oil	1½ teaspoons vegetable oil	60
salt and pepper	salt and pepper	
1 spring onion	1 scallion	2
1 stick celery	1 stalk celery	5
2 oz (50g) green or red pepper	2 ounces green or red pepper	8
a few lettuce leaves	a few lettuce leaves	
		213

Cook the potatoes until tender. (Peel the potatoes at this stage if preferred.) Cool and dice. In a liquidizer blend the tofu, lemon juice and oil. Add seasoning to taste. Chop the spring onion (scallion), celery and pepper finely. Add the potatoes and the tofu dressing and mix thoroughly. Serve on a bed of lettuce.

Dinner

SPAGHETTI WITH TEMPEH AND MUSHROOM SAUCE

Imperial (Metric)	American	Calories
1 tablespoon Tamari (soya sauce)	1 tablespoon Tamari (soy sauce)	5
2 tablespoons water	2 tablespoons water	
4 oz (100g) tempeh	4 ounces tempeh	157
2 teaspoons vegetable oil	2 teaspoons vegetable oil	80
1 small onion	1 small onion	
1 small clove garlic	1 small clove garlic	14
2 oz (50g) mushrooms	1 cup mushrooms	5
4 oz (100g) tomatoes	4 ounces tomatoes	16
1 tablespoon tomato purée	1 tablespoon tomato paste	
1 teaspoon dried basil	1 teaspoon sweet basil	
2 oz (50g) wholemeal spaghetti	2 ounces wholewheat spaghetti	200
		477
	Total	950

Heat the Tamari and water in a small saucepan. Put the tempeh into the pan, lower heat, cover pan and leave to simmer 5-7 minutes. Turn over and cook on the other side for a further 5-7 minutes. Meanwhile, chop the onion and crush the garlic. Heat the oil in a larger saucepan and *sauté* the onion and garlic until softened. Skin and chop the tomatoes. Chop the mushrooms. Add both to the saucepan, along with the tomato *purée* (paste) and basil. Stir well. Empty the contents of the small saucepan into the larger one, mashing the tempeh with a fork while doing so. Mix well. Cover pan and simmer for about 15 minutes, stirring occasionally. Meanwhile, cook the spaghetti, drain it, and pour the sauce over it.

MENU 12

Breakfast

Imperial (Metric)	American	Calories
small passion fruit	small passion fruit	10

CREAMY OATMEAL PORRIDGE

Imperial (Metric)	American	Calories
8 fl oz (225ml) skimmed milk or 6 fl oz (175ml) soya milk diluted with 2 fl oz (50ml) water	1 cup skim milk or ¾ cup soy milk diluted with ¼ cup water	75
1 oz (25g) porridge oats	¼ cup rolled oats	100
2 teaspoons raw sugar	2 teaspoons raw sugar	34
		219

Slice the passion fruit in half and eat the inside with a teaspoon. To make the porridge heat the milk gently and stir in the oats. Bring to the boil, then simmer for about 3 minutes. Serve topped with sugar.

Lunch

CURRIED RICE SALAD*

Imperial (Metric)	American	Calories
2 oz (50g) brown rice	⅓ cup brown rice	200
1 stick celery	1 stalk celery	5
2 oz (50g) mushrooms	1 cup mushrooms	5
1 small onion	1 small onion	12
½ oz (15g) peanuts	½ ounce peanuts	80
3 oz (75g) dairy or soya yogurt	⅓ cup dairy or soy yogurt	45
½-1 teaspoon curry powder	½-1 teaspoon curry powder	
½ teaspoon soya sauce	½ teaspoon soy sauce	
		347

*A version of this recipe first appeared in *Green Cuisine* magazine (September/October, 1986).

Cook the rice and cool it (or use previously cooked rice). Slice the celery and mushrooms. Chop the onion finely. Mix with the rice, along with the peanuts. Beat the curry powder and soya sauce into the yogurt until creamy. Pour over the rice and mix in well. Taste for seasoning. Serve immediately or chill briefly in the refrigerator first.

Dinner

VEGETABLE CHARLOTTE WITH SMOKED TOFU

Imperial (Metric)	American	Calories
1 small carrot	1 small carrot	12
2 oz (50g) Brussels sprouts	2 ounces Brussels sprouts	14
1 small onion	1 small onion	12
4 oz (100g) potatoes	¼ pound potatoes	100
¼ pint (150ml) water	⅔ cup water	
2 teaspoons vegetable oil	2 teaspoons vegetable oil	80
½ oz (15g) wholemeal flour	⅛ cup wholewheat flour	50
salt and pepper	salt and pepper	
4 oz (100g) smoked tofu	¼ pound smoked tofu	116
1 oz (25g) wholemeal breadcrumbs	½ cup wholewheat breadcrumbs	65
		449
	Total	1015

Chop the carrot, sprouts and onion fairly coarsely. Chop the potato finely. Put the vegetables into a saucepan. Cover with the water, bring to the boil, then lower heat, cover pan, and simmer until the vegetables are just cooked (10-15 minutes). Meanwhile, slice the tofu fairly thinly and grill (broil) on both sides until lightly golden. Drain the vegetables, retaining the stock. Heat the oil in a saucepan and stir in the flour, then add the vegetable stock, stirring well to avoid lumps. Season to taste. Stir in the vegetables. Transfer the vegetables to a heat-proof dish or casserole. Place the slices of tofu on top. Sprinkle on the breadcrumbs. Place under the grill (broiler) for a minute or two to crisp up the crumbs, and serve immediately.

MENU 13

Breakfast

Imperial (Metric)	American	Calories
2 oz (50g) grapes	2 ounces grapes	30

OATCAKES WITH STRAWBERRY TAHINI

Imperial (Metric)	American	Calories
½ oz (15g) tahini	½ ounce tahini	85
2 teaspoons raw sugar or sugar-free strawberry jam	2 teaspoons raw sugar or sugar-free strawberry jam	34
3 oatcakes	3 oatcakes	180
		329

Mix the tahini with the jam and spread on the oatcakes.

Lunch

FRENCH ONION SOUP

Imperial (Metric)	American	Calories
1 medium or 2 small onions	1 medium or 2 small onions	24
2 teaspoons vegetable margarine	2 teaspoons vegetable margarine	80
8 fl oz (225ml) water	1 cup water	
1 teaspoon yeast extract	1 teaspoon yeast extract	10
1 small slice wholemeal bread	1 small slice wholewheat bread	65
2 teaspoons Parmesan cheese or nutritional yeast	2 teaspoons Parmesan cheese or nutritional yeast	25
		204

Slice the onions thinly. Heat the margarine in a small saucepan, add the onions, and *sauté* slowly until golden. Add the water and yeast extract, bring to the boil, and simmer for about 15 minutes, then transfer the soup to a heatproof bowl. Toast the slice of bread. Break it into large pieces and put them on top of the soup. Sprinkle with the cheese or yeast, and place under a grill (broiler) for a couple of minutes until beginning to brown. Serve immediately.

Dinner

LENTIL TOMATO ROAST

Imperial (Metric)	American	Calories
2 oz (50g) red lentils	⅓ cup red lentils	160
1 small onion	1 small onion	12
¼ pint (150ml) water	⅔ cup water	
1½ oz (40g) wholemeal breadcrumbs	¾ cup wholewheat breadcrumbs	95
¼ teaspoon yeast extract	¼ teaspoon yeast extract	
2 teaspoons vegetable margarine	2 teaspoons vegetable margarine	80
1 tablespoon tomato purée	1 tablespoon tomato paste	10
½ teaspoon dried basil	½ teaspoon sweet basil	
1 small tomato	1 small tomato	10
4 oz (100g) potatoes	¼ pound potatoes	100
4 oz (100g) Brussels sprouts	¼ pound Brussels sprouts	28
		495
	Total	1028

Wash the lentils well. Chop the onion finely. Place the lentils and onion in a saucepan, and cover with the water. Bring to the boil, then lower heat, cover pan, and simmer for about 15 minutes, by which time the lentils should be very soft. Remove from heat and add the breadcrumbs, yeast extract, margarine, tomato *purée* (paste) and basil. Mix well and turn into an oven dish. Slice the tomato thinly and place the slices on top of the roast. Bake at 350°F (180°C/Gas Mark 4) for about half an hour. Serve accompanied by boiled or baked potatoes and lightly-steamed Brussels sprouts.

'CRASH' DIETS

It is generally agreed by dietitians that calories are burned more efficiently, and more rapid weight loss achieved, if small amounts are eaten during the day instead of in three separate meals. The suggestions which follow do not aim to be much below 1000 calories, but these calories are spread out instead of being consumed in three sittings. They are not meant to be kept up for long periods at a time, though the combination of fresh and dried fruit with nuts or seeds is energizing, sustaining and nutritious. The diets are particularly useful for days when you have not time or cannot be bothered to prepare meals but want to continue losing weight.

FRUIT AND NUTS

Imperial (Metric)	American	Calories
3 oz (75g) almonds	¾ cup almonds	480
3 oz (75g) dates or raisins	½ cup dates or raisins	250
5 pieces of fresh fruit (apple, pear, orange or banana)	5 pieces of fresh fruit (apple, pear, orange or banana)	250
		980

Divide nuts and dried fruit into five portions and eat with fresh fruit at regular intervals.

FRUIT AND NUT BALLS

Imperial (Metric)	American	Calories
2 oz (50g) raisins	⅓ cup raisins	140
2 oz (50g) figs	⅓ cup chopped figs	120
2 oz (50g) dried apricots	⅓ cup chopped dried apricots	100
2 oz (50g) almonds	½ cup almonds	320
6 pieces fresh fruit	6 pieces fresh fruit	300
		980

Put first three ingredients through a mincer, a handful of each in turn. Then put through again with nuts. Form into 12 small balls and eat them two at a time on 6 different occasions with a piece of fruit (apple, pear, orange or banana).

HAWAIIAN SPECIAL

Imperial (Metric)	American	Calories
1 pint (600ml) unsweetened pineapple juice	2½ cups unsweetened pineapple juice	320
1½ oz (40g) sunflower seeds	⅓ cup sunflower seeds	255
1 ripe banana	1 ripe banana	50
1½ oz (40g) dates or raisins	¼ cup dates or raisins	100
1 oz (25g) sesame seeds	⅙ cup sesame seeds	160
1 large grated apple	1 large grated apple	60
		945

Liquidize all ingredients very thoroughly and refrigerate. Drink a small cupful whenever you feel hungry.

DESSERTS

HONEY GLAZED PEAR

Imperial (Metric)	American	Calories
1 pear	1 pear	50
2 teaspoons honey	2 teaspoons honey	40
rind and juice of half an orange	rind and juice of half an orange	25
		115

Peel pear and simmer in water until almost soft. Drain. Mix orange rind and honey in pan and bring to boil. Place pear in juice and cook gently for 10-15 minutes until soft. Turn occasionally. Remove pear. Boil juice for a minute longer, pour over pear and serve.

BAKED PEACH

Imperial (Metric)	American	Calories
1 peach	1 peach	40
2 teaspoons brown sugar	2 teaspoons brown sugar	34
1 teaspoon lemon juice	1 teaspoon lemon juice	
½ teaspoon vegetable margarine	½ teaspoon vegetable margarine	20
		94

Cut off about an inch of skin from both ends of peach. Set it in a baking dish, sprinkle with lemon juice and sugar, and dot with margarine. Bake in a 350°F (180°C/Gas Mark 4) oven for about 20 minutes. Serve hot or cold.

HONEY MARINATED STRAWBERRIES

Imperial (Metric)	American	Calories
half an orange	half an orange	25
dash of almond essence	dash of almond essence	
½ teaspoon arrowroot	½ teaspoon arrowroot	5
2 teaspoons honey	2 teaspoons honey	40
4 oz (100g) fresh strawberries	¼ pound fresh strawberries	25
		95

Squeeze juice from orange and blend in honey. Add essence. Hull strawberries and leave to soak in the mixture for half an hour. Drain and place in serving dish. Measure the marinade and add enough cold water to make 3 fl oz (75ml/just under ½ cup). Bring to the boil and stir in arrowroot which has been mixed with about a teaspoon of water. Leave to cool and pour over strawberries.

APPLE MOULD

Imperial (Metric)	American	Calories
4 oz (100g) cooking apples	¼ pound soft tart apples	30
½ teaspoon powdered agar-agar	½ teaspoon powdered agar-agar	
1 tablespoon raw sugar or sugar-free strawberry, raspberry or apricot jam	1 tablespoon raw sugar or sugar-free strawberry, raspberry or apricot jam	50
		80

Peel, core and slice apple. Cook with jam and 1-2 tablespoons water until very soft. Add the agar-agar and simmer together for a few minutes. Pour into wetted mould. Turn out when set.

IMITATION ALMOND MOULD

Imperial (Metric)	American	Calories
¼ pint (150ml) skimmed milk or 4 fl oz (100ml) soya milk diluted with 1 fl oz (25ml) water	⅔ cup skim milk or ½ cup soymilk diluted with ⅛ cup water	50
1 tablespoon wholemeal semolina	1 tablespoon wholewheat farina	35
1 teaspoon powdered agar-agar	1 teaspoon powdered agar-agar	
1 tablespoon brown sugar	1 tablespoon brown sugar	50
½ teaspoon almond essence	½ teaspoon almond essence	
1 teaspoon raw sugar or sugar-free raspberry or cherry jam	1 teaspoon raw sugar or sugar-free raspberry or cherry jam	17
		152

Bring milk to the boil, sprinkle in semolina (farina), simmer for 3-4 minutes, stirring occasionally. Stir in agar-agar and simmer for a minute or two longer. Remove from heat. Add sugar and almond essence. Rinse mould with cold water, place jam at the bottom, cover with mixture. Leave to cool, then place in refrigerator to chill. Turn out when set.

FRUITY YOGURT

Imperial (Metric)	American	Calories
3 fl oz (75g) dairy or soya yogurt	⅓ cup dairy or soy yogurt	45
4 oz (100g) fresh cherries	¼ pound fresh cherries	45
1 teaspoon honey	1 teaspoon honey	20
		110

Mix yogurt with honey. Stone cherries and mix in well. Chill and serve.

VEGETARIAN WHOLEFOOD CALORIE CHART

Breads and Biscuits	Calories per ounce
Wholemeal (wholewheat) bread	64
Sweet or savoury biscuits (cookies or crackers)	120-140
Crispbreads (per slice):	
Starch-reduced crispbread	21-24
Primula rye, extra thin	17
Kelloggs Scanda-Brod Brown	32
Scanda Crisp	19
Ryvita — light or brown	26
Rye King Light	28
Rye King Brown	35

Cereals and Grains	Calories per ounce
Muesli	100-110
Granola-type cereals	130-140
Oats, uncooked	112
Weetabix, Grapenuts, Shredded Wheat	100

Cereals and Grains	Calories per ounce
Wheat Germ	100
Cornflakes	104
Wholemeal flour	100
Millet	100
Spaghetti, macaroni, noodles	100

Dairy Produce	Calories per ounce
Cheeses:	
Camembert cheese	88
Cream cheese	230
Cheddar	120
Danish Blue	103
Edam	88
Gouda	96
Gruyère	132
Parmesan	118
Whole milk	19
Skimmed milk	10
Double cream	131
Single cream	62
Butter	226
Yogurt (plain low fat)	12-16
Eggs	46

Fruit	Calories per ounce
Apple, orange, peach	10
Apricots, fresh	7
Apricots, dried	52
Avocado pear	25
Banana	22
Berries	7
Cherries	11
Dates	70
Figs	61
Grapes, black	14
Grapes, white	17
Grapefruit, melon, soft fruit	6
Lemon, gooseberries	4
Passion fruit	4
Pear	9
Plum	12
Pineapple, fresh	12
Pineapple, tinned (canned) in juice	14
Raisins	70
Sultanas	71
Tangerine	7

Juices	Calories per ounce
Apple	10
Carrot	12
Grape	19
Orange	10
Lemon, grapefruit	9
Pineapple	15
Tomato	6
V8 Vegetable	6

Nuts and Seeds	Calories per ounce
Almonds	160
Brazils	180
Cashews	178
Chestnut	49
Desiccated coconut	178
Hazelnuts	181
Peanuts	171
Peanut Butter	180
Walnuts	150
Sunflower seeds	170
Sesame seeds	161

Pulses	Calories per ounce
Baked beans (canned vegetarian baked beans)	25
Black-eyed beans (peas)	85
Lentils (raw)	80
Butter (Lima) beans (raw)	90
Butter (Lima) beans (cooked)	26
Chick peas (Garbanzo beans) (raw)	90
Chick peas (Garbanzo beans) (cooked)	33
Red kidney beans (raw)	90
Red kidney beans (cooked)	33

Soya (Soy) Foods	Calories per ounce
Soya (Soy) sauce	20
Soya (Soy) milk	12
Tempeh	39
Tofu (firm)	29
Tofu (silken)	13
TVP (raw)	95

	Calories per ounce
Sugar and Sweeteners	
Black treacle (molasses)	75
Honey	82
Jam	74
Sugar	112
Fats and Oils	
Margarine	210
Oils	254
Vegetables (uncooked)	
Asparagus, green beans	5
Aubergine (eggplant), broccoli, cauliflower, courgette (zucchini), green and red peppers, radish, spinach, watercress	4

	Calories per ounce
Vegetables (uncooked)	
Broad (Windsor) beans, beetroot (beet)	13
Brussels sprouts	7
Cabbage, carrot, onion swede (rutabaga),	6
Celery, mushrooms	2
Chicory, cucumber, mustard and cress, lettuce	3
Leek	9
Mung bean sprouts	5
Parsnips	14
Peas	15
Potatoes	25
Sweetcorn (corn)	22
Tomatoes (fresh)	4
Tomatoes (tinned/canned)	3

INDEX